To Lynette + Bob
Hope you enjoy this
visit to Canada -
without leaving your
easy chair -
Merry Christmas 1995

George

MW01671237

O Canada

Its geography,

Swallowtail Lighthouse
Grand Manan, New Brunswick

history,

Canoe Manned by Voyageurs Passing a Waterfall, Francis Anne Hopkins

and the people

multicultu[illegible] celebration in Winnipeg, Manitoba

who call it home.

Vancouveratnight

Three oceans, millions of lakes, vast plains, virgin forests, the Rockies, the shores of the St. Lawrence River and four well-defined seasons: these gifts from the gods form a great nation. Add to them a soul sculpted by three thousand years of Amerindian, Greco-Latin and western culture, and the result is Canada, a shining hour in the history of the world.

—Antonine Maillet

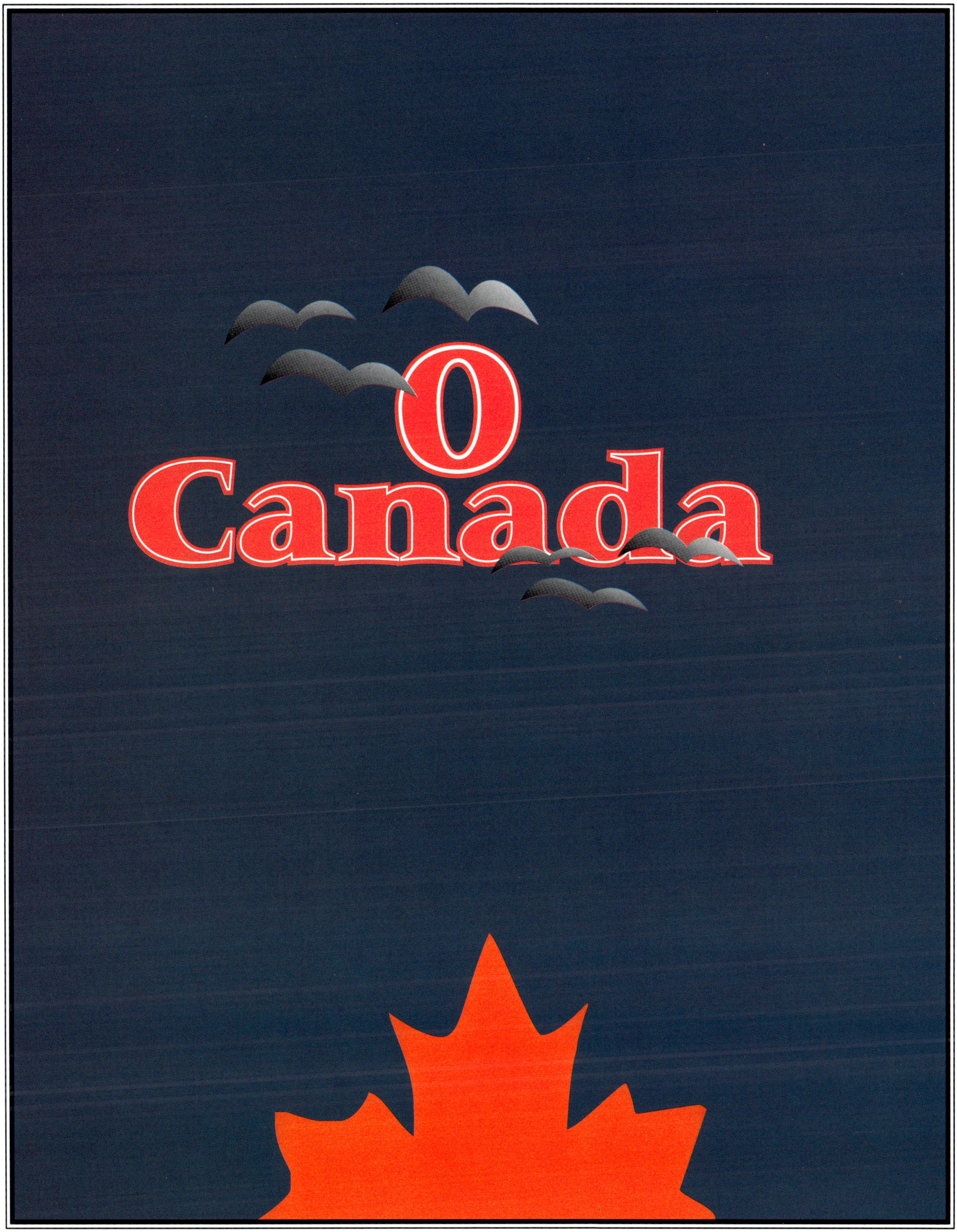
O
Canada

This book was typeset and designed on a Macintosh IIsi computer
using the following software packages:

word processing: *Microsoft Word*

charts & Graphs: *DeltaGraph*

maps: *MapArt* customized in *Aldus FreeHand*

illustrations: *Aldus FreeHand*

layout: *Aldus PageMaker*

---

text, maps, illustrations, layout and graphic design by **George Sherman**

archival & other photos collected by **George Sherman**, edited with **Richard Beach**

charts researched and prepared by **David Backus**

final copy edited by **Mary Williams**

index by **Deborah Whiteman**

Printed by **BENCHEMARK PRINTING** Schenectady, NY

O Canada

its geography, history and the people who call it home

designed and written by GEORGE SHERMAN

managing editor: RICHARD BEACH

1995

published by the Center for the Study of Canada

State University of New York, Plattsburgh

CLASSROOM CONSULTANTS

Roy S. Cichoski, Camels Hump Middle School, Richmond, VT
Kathy Douglas, Ferrisburgh Central School, Ferrisburgh, VT
Virginia M. Figura, Franklinville Central School, Franklinville, NY
Carol-Ann Harris, Franklin Middle School, Nutley, NJ
Jack Hornung, Sweet Home High, Amherst, NY
Sandra S. Kessler, Thornell Road Elementary, Pittsford, NY
Dr. T. Joseph McGrath, Fairfield Woods Middle School, Fairfield, CT
Dorothy F. Osterhout, Johnsburg Central School, North Creek, NY
Colin M. Ramsay, Hillsborough Community College, Tampa, FL.
Karen Scofield, Garanda Central School, Walworth, NY
Donald Stear, Marion Center Area High School, Marion Center, PA
Ruth Ann Writer, Buchanan High School, Buchanan, MI
Donna J. Young, Onondaga Nation School, Nedrow, NY
William E. Young, Clyde Junior High, Clyde, OH

SPECIAL THANKS TO

- Harcourt Brace Jovanovich for their cooperation. Several chapters of this book were originally written to be part of a textbook on North America the company planned to publish. When their priorities changed, the company graciously agreed to return the manuscript to the Center for the Study of Canada so it could be broadened, illustrated and published as a Canadian Studies text. Thanks for early guidance and support go to **Thomas Williamson**, Director, HBJ School Department; **Donald P. Lankiewicz**, Director of Elementary Social Studies; **Patty Hosley**, Executive Editor, Elementary Social Studies and **Douglas E. Hawthorne**, Senior Editor.

- the Public Archives of Canada, especially **Hélène Godda** and **Ronne Mokhtar**, Reference and Researcher Services Division, Public Programs Branch.

- the Canadian Consulate General, New York for its assistance and support, especially to **John McNeil**, Academic Relations Officer and **Ann Garneau**, Consul for Culture and Academic Affairs.

- **Herb Carpenter** and Northeast Printing of Plattsburgh, NY for their shipping services and printing of publicity materials, the teacher's guide and companion children's literature collection.

- **Bob Kosineski, Jr.** for his enthusiastic support and printing expertise—and to the other talented people at Benchemark Printing, Schenectady, New York.

- The wizard **Nadine Balzer** for her technical support and expertise and to **U-Compute**, Plattsburgh, NY.

- **Mary Williams** for her excellent work as final copy reader and to indexer **Deborah Whiteman**.

- to staff members at the Center for the Study of Canada, SUNY Plattsburgh, for their invaluable assistance: **Lois Bouvier**, **Lynn Bouvier**, **Greg James** and student intern, **David Backus** who researched and prepared most of the charts and graphs that appear in *O Canada*.

and to the following agencies and individuals who supplied photographic images

Assembly of First Nations • Calgary Convention and Visitors Bureau • Canadian Consulate General
Canadian Embassy • Canadian Heritage • Dennis Hulbert • Government of Canada, Deparment of Foreign Affairs
Government of Saskatchewan Photographic Services Agency • Hydro-Québec • Inco Limited
Maclean's Magazino • Metropolitan Toronto Convention & Visitors Association • Ministère du tourisme du Québec
National Film Board of Canada • Nova Scotia Tourism • Ontario Ministry of Tourism and Recreation
NWT Economic Development and Tourism • Orest Semchishen • Ottawa Tourism and Convention Authority
PEI Tourism • Petro-Canada • Petroleum Communication Foundation • Public Archives of Canada (PAC)
Richard Beach • Toronto Blue Jays • Tourism British Columbia • Tourism New Brunswick
Tourism Vancouver • Travel Manitoba • United Press Canada Limited
University of Washington • Wayne Sturge (Government of Newfoundland and Labrador)
West Edmonton Mall • Yukon Government

Copyright © 1995 Center for the Study of Canada, State University of New York, Plattsburgh

All rights reserved. No part of this book may be reproduced or transmitted in any form or by any means, electronic or mechanical, including photocopying, recording, or by any information storage and retrieval system, without permission in writing from the publisher.

Center for the Study of Canada
133 Court Street, SUNY Plattsburgh
Plattsburgh, NY 12901

Printed in the United States of America

ISBN 1-885468-00-8

Library of Congress Catalog Card Number 94-71904

the author, editor and publisher

GEORGE SHERMAN is a secondary social studies teacher and is the Associate for Educational Outreach at the Center for the Study of Canada, SUNY Plattsburgh where he has been co-editor of *Teaching Canada*, a newsletter for teachers, since 1982. He has written numerous articles about Canada and Canadian Studies as well as two other books, *The Canada Connection in American History* and *Teaching About the Canadian Parliamentary System.* He was also scriptwriter for *The Canadian Parliamentary Video*, a cooperative effort of the University of the State of New York and the Canadian Broadcasting Corporation. He has conducted many workshops on Canadian Studies for teachers across the northeastern United States.

RICHARD BEACH is special editorial consultant and managing editor for this book. He has been the Director of the Center for the Study of Canada at the State University of New York, Plattsburgh, since 1975. Dr. Beach has written numerous articles and several books and historical atlases on Canada and North America in his fields of cultural geography and Canadian Studies. Before becoming a university professor in 1970, he taught for several years in the public schools of Quebec. He is a past President of the Association for Canadian Studies in the United States.

THE CENTER FOR THE STUDY OF CANADA, at the State University of New York, Plattsburgh manages the most comprehensive undergraduate program in Canadian Studies in the United States, sponsors numerous seminars and workshops for university professors and teachers from around the world and directs an extensive outreach program to elementary and secondary schools. This book is one of the Center's many resources on Canada designed for use in American schools. Others include teaching and resource guides, posters, videos and a free biannual newsletter.

reviewers

Donald Alper
Professor of Political Science
Director, Center for Canadian Studies
Western Washington University, Bellingham, Washington

Michael Bittner
Outreach Coordinator, Canadian Studies Center
The Henry M. Jackson School of International Studies
University of Washington, Seattle, Washington.

Les Buell
Social Studies Teacher
Williamson Central School, Williamson, New York

Barbara Foster
Social Studies Teacher
Rock Lake Middle School, Longwood, Florida

Ted Henson
Director of Elementary School Education
Alamance Country Schools, Graham, North Carolina

Jack Hotchkiss
Teacher
Scotia-Glenville Children's Museum, Scotia, New York

William Joyce
Professor of Education and Director of Canadian Studies
Michigan State University, Lansing, Michigan

Henry Kennedy
Professsor of Political Science
Director, Canadian Studies Program
University of Central Florida, Orlando, Florida

Jeanne Kissner
Professor of French
Associate Director, Center for the Study of Canada
SUNY Plattsburgh, Plattsburgh, New York

Patrice LeClerc
Coordinator of Canadian Studies
Duke University, Durham, North Carolina

Barry Lepler
Social Studies Teacher
Norup Middle School
Oak Park, Michigan

Charles LeWarne
Social Studies Teacher and Historian (retired)
Edmonds, Washington

William Metcalfe
Professor of History
Director, Canadian Studies Program
University of Vermont, Burlington, Vermont

Robert Monahan
Professor of Geography
Director, Canadian Studies Program
Western Washington University, Bellingham, Washington

Michael Peterman
Professor of English
Editor, *Journal of Canadian Studies*
Trent University
Peterborough, Ontario

Marion Salinger
Canadian Studies Consultant and Author
Durham, North Carolina

John Herd Thompson
Professor of History
Duke University, Durham, North Carolina

Christine Turrone
Grade 5 Teacher
Overlook Elementary School, Poughkeepsie, New York

Judith Wooster
Assistant Superintendent of Schools,
Bethlehem Central Schools, Delmar, New York

Bernard Yvon
Professor of Education
University of Maine, Orono, Maine

Gail Yvon
Outreach Coordinator
Canadian-American Center
University of Maine, Orono, Maine

TEACHER'S GUIDE by **Christine Turrone and Peggy Hansen** • CHILDREN'S LITERATURE SUPPLEMENT **by Emily Castine**

O Canada

TABLE OF CONTENTS

maps

charts & graphs

SASKATCHEWAN
POOL
CRAVEN

UNIT 2 *a child of warring parents*

THE HISTORY OF CANADA

UNIT 3 *a country divided by geography*

THE PEOPLE AND PLACES OF CANADA

Beaufort Sea
ALASKA (United States)
Victoria Island
Dawson
YUKON TERRITORY
Whitehorse
Great Bear Lake
Pacific Ocean
Great Slave Lake
Yellowknife
NORTHWEST TERRITORIES
Lake Athabasca
BRITISH COLUMBIA
ALBERTA
Churchill
Edmonton
SASKATCHEWAN
MANITOBA
Victoria
Vancouver
Calgary
Saskatoon
Lake Winnipeg
Regina
Winnipeg
Thunder
UNITED STATES
Calgary
City
International Boundary
Provincial Boundary
Province Name
500 km
0
500 Miles

CANADA
GREENLAND
(Denmark)
ICELAND
Baffin Bay
Baffin
Island
Hudson
Bay
James
Bay
Labrador
Sea
NEWFOUNDLAND
St.
John's
QUEBEC
ONTARIO
Gulf of St. Lawrence
Charlottetown
PRINCE
EDWARD
ISLAND
Sydney
NOVA SCOTIA
NEW
BRUNSWICK
St. Lawrence
River
Fredericton
Saint John
Halifax
Quebec
Montreal
Superior
Ottawa
Lake Huron
Toronto
Lake
Ontario
Lake
Michigan
Lake
Erie
Atlantic
Ocean

introduction

Canada and the United States are good neighbors and have many things in common. Both countries are large, scenic and rich in natural resources. Both are democracies. Canadians and Americans enjoy many of the same books and movies and watch many of the same television programs. It is no wonder that millions of people from Canada and the United States cross the border every year as tourists, shoppers, workers and students.

Still, for all their similarities, Canada and the United States are different in a number of important ways. For one thing, one quarter of the Canadian people are French speaking. The French language can be seen and heard in most of the country. Another important difference is that there are only one-tenth as many Canadians as Americans. Four of every five Canadians live within 100 miles of the Canada-United States border. By contrast, most Americans live a long way from Canada.

Canadians and Americans purchase millions of dollars worth of each other's products every day. Canada has an abundance of natural resources such as oil and fresh water that are in increasingly short supply in the United States. And American factories produce many products that Canadians buy. In fact, Canadians buy more American-made products than the people of any other country. Americans return the favor by purchasing more products from Canada than from anywhere else.

As the 21st century approaches, the leaders of both Canada and the United States know how important each country is to the other. After reading the pages in this book, you will know, too.

UNIT 1

the geography of Canada

A PLACE OF INCREDIBLE SPACE

It is impossible to know this country without having wintered there. On arriving in summer, everything was very pleasant . . . but winter in this country lasts six months.

These words were written by Samuel de Champlain nearly 400 years ago during one of his many journeys along the St. Lawrence River. Champlain was one of the most widely traveled and most observant of the European explorers of North America. He was not the first person, nor the last, to be impressed with Canada's geography and climate. The extremes of both have helped shape the country.

Canada is the second largest country in the world with nearly four million square miles. It extends northward from its southern border with the United States almost to the North Pole, a distance of 3,000 miles. From east to west, Canada measures more than 4,500 miles and stretches across six time zones.

Canada is blessed with an abundance of natural beauty and natural resources. Within its boundaries lie huge expanses of fertile plains, lush green forests and icy white landscapes, thousands of towering mountains and more than a million bodies of fresh water. Beneath its surface lies a treasure-chest of mineral resources including nickel, uranium, iron, copper, silver, gold, oil and natural gas. Canada's abundant natural wealth is one of many reasons why this country is so important to the United States.

ESSAY Geography and Canadian culture

A "loonie," Canada's one dollar coin.

Because it is so awesome and so challenging, the geography of Canada has left its mark on Canadian culture.

From the red maple leaf on their national flag to the furry beavers and graceful loons carved on their coins, Canadians love the symbols of their wilderness—even if the only landscape most of them see in their everyday lives is that of the country's modern cities.

The harshness of the climate and geography touches almost every aspect of life in Canada. The challenges posed by wilderness and weather are important themes in much of the country's art and literature. They are also the main reasons why 80 percent of Canadians choose to live in the southern reaches of their country.

Canadians seem to have a love-hate relationship with their winters. Their fashion and sports, their modes of construction and transportation, are shaped by their efforts to deal with the cold—both to cope with it and to enjoy it.

The production of winter clothing and footwear, especially beautiful leather boots and coats, are an important part of the Canadian fashion industry. Bright parkas and colorful scarves and mittens are important elements of the wardrobes of most Canadians for nearly half the year.

Even though the man who invented basketball was born in Canada, most Canadians would much rather play and watch hockey—maybe because the icy playing surface makes it seem more Canadian. American youngsters look forward all winter to summer days on the baseball diamond. Young Canadians enjoy baseball, too, but a lot of them look forward more eagerly to that first freezing day in November when they can lace up a pair of skates and head for the nearest patch of ice. Sledding, snowmobiling, skiing and snowboarding are other favorite winter pastimes that take advantage of the ice and snow.

Geography and wildlife are favorite themes in Canadian art and literature, especially in the works of native Canadian artists such as Norval Morrisseau, who created this drawing entitled Peter and his Friends.

Most Canadians who follow professional sports, including baseball and football, watch games in modern indoor stadiums. After the game, shopping, supper and even the subway ride home may all take place underground in one of the mall-like centers built beneath the streets of several Canadian cities.

While winter is a harsh reality for almost all of Canada, it is not the only season. In the places most Canadians live, spring brings warm temperatures that encourage the grass to grow green and the trees to bud. Other joys of spring include brightly colored flowers and delicious maple syrup. During the summer, many places in southern Canada can be uncomfortably hot with daytime temperatures often reaching to between 80° and 90° Fahrenheit from June through August.

No need for a raincheck at Toronto's SkyDome, where baseball can be played indoors.

Canadians make the most of their warm weather. Long summer vacations are common. Many city dwellers own cottages in the countryside and spend their summer leisure time enjoying the quiet and beauty of the lake-filled wilderness.

September and October are also pleasant from coast to coast in southern Canada. The air is cool and crisp and often the skies are filled with flocks of geese and other birds heading south for the winter. In the countryside, leaves change from deep green to brilliant shades of yellow, orange and red. Among them are the maple leaves that Canadians have adopted as the symbol of their country. ■

CHAPTER 1

The Natural Regions of Canada

Steep-walled tidal inlets are found along most of the waterways that lead to the interior of New Brunswick.

Puffins, with their bright orange beaks and bulging white tummies, are one of many wildlife species native to Atlantic Canada.

TO GUIDE YOUR READING
Look for answers to these questions

1 What is a natural region?

2 What are Canada's natural regions?

3 In what ways are the natural regions of Canada different from one another?

INTRODUCTION

Geographers love to study Canada because it has some of the most unusual and impressive landscapes found on earth.

*Since Canada contains more than 8 percent of the world's land surface, it is not surprising that the country is made up of many different **natural regions**. Natural regions are areas of the earth's surface that are defined by their geography. There are six natural regions in Canada.*

*Geographers use the term **regional diversity** to describe countries like Canada that contain many different natural regions within their borders.*

THE APPALACHIAN REGION

The Appalachian Region is located in southeastern Canada. The eastern edge of this region is often referred to as **Atlantic Canada** because its islands, peninsulas and coastal shores are washed by the Atlantic Ocean.

The natural landscape is varied. Lowland coastal

areas and fertile valleys are shadowed by the low mountains of the **Appalachian Mountain System**. Most of the region is covered with large expanses of dense forest. There are, however, many green fields and sandy beaches near the coastal areas, and that is where most of the region's people make their homes.

The waters along Canada's Atlantic coast are shallow. The ocean floor here was once a part of the mainland before the ocean levels rose thousands of years ago. The most shallow ocean area is known as the **Grand Banks**, a huge, flat underground ledge that provides an ideal environment for fish to breed and grow. During the 1600s, schools of fish in these waters were so thick that they actually slowed the ships of early explorers bound for North America.

Many of the first French and English settlements in Canada were temporary fishing camps built along the shores of the Atlantic region more than 400 years ago. Each winter, the fishermen folded their nets and headed back to Europe to wait for spring. Fishing, including lobstering, is still one of the most important economic activities in the region.

The Cape Tryon Lighthouse on Prince Edward Island is one of many found throughout Atlantic Canada. They were built to help captains find their way along the shoreline at night.

the story of tides

Oceans are affected by the pull of the moon's gravity. The strength of the pull changes as the Earth rotates, causing the ocean waters to rise and fall. As they do, shorelines change from morning to night. Maximum and minimum pull occurs in six-hour cycles. These pictures of the Minas Basin, Nova Scotia were taken only a few hours apart. The top photo was taken at high tide. Below, the ocean has retreated, leaving boats in the basin high and dry at low tide. Tidal ranges in Atlantic Canada are among the greatest in the world—57 feet in one part of the Bay of Fundy.

Prince Edward Island is a popular destination for vacationers, largely because of the island's many miles of sandy beaches.

Sadly, the number of fish, especially cod, has declined drastically during recent years. One reason for this is that larger and larger boats, both Canadian and foreign, have taken too many fish from these waters in too short a time.

Other economic activities in the Appalachian Region include forestry, farming and coal mining. Tourism is important, too. The region's unspoiled natural beauty makes it a popular spot for vacationers from other parts of Canada and from other countries as well—especially the United States.

The region's few cities are quite small when compared with cities like Montreal or Toronto. **Halifax**, Nova Scotia is the largest of these cities, with a population of 200,000. Located on the Atlantic coast, it has always been an important center of trade because its port is located in a sheltered inlet that is free of ice all year long. It has also long been headquarters for the Canadian Navy.

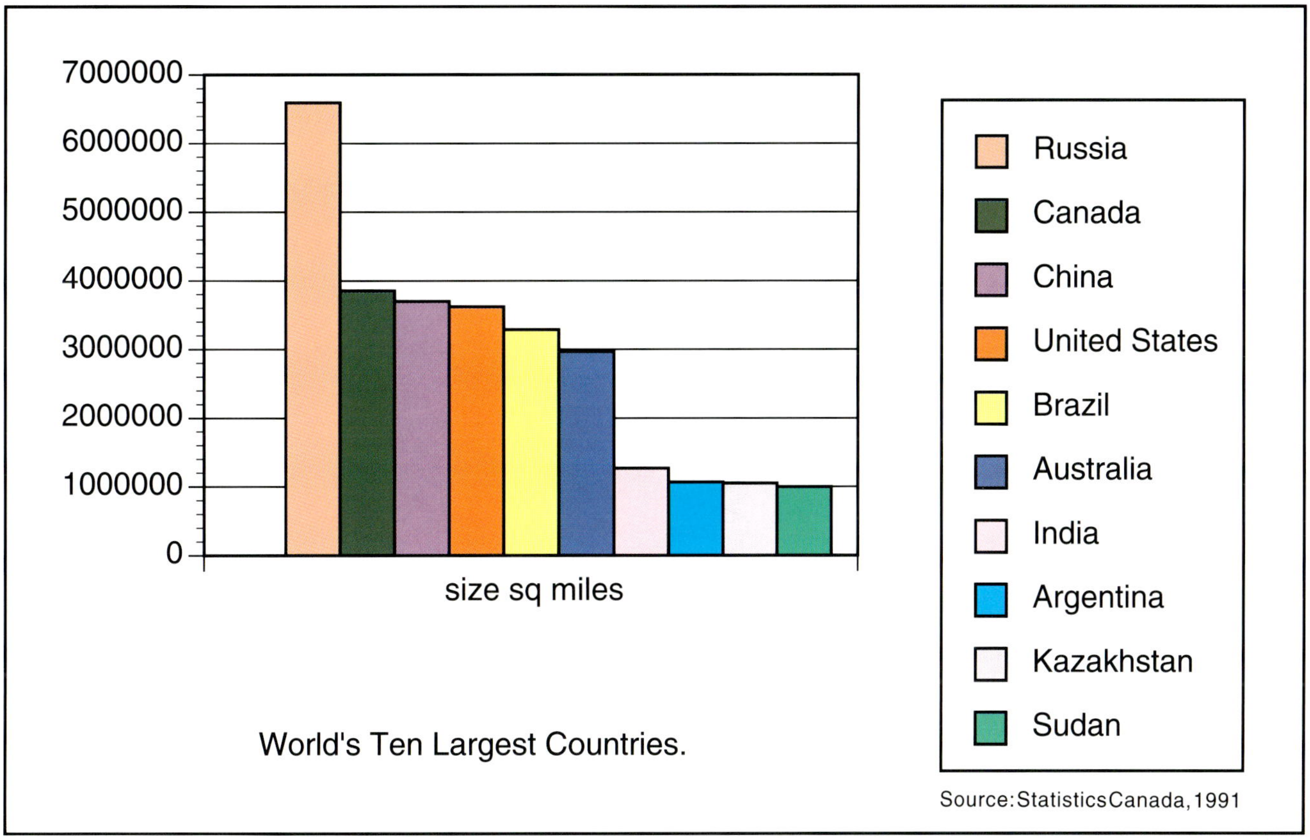

THE ST. LAWRENCE/GREAT LAKES LOWLANDS REGION

The St. Lawrence/Great Lakes Lowlands Region is the smallest natural region in Canada, but it is the most heavily populated. Located inland from the Atlantic Ocean, the region extends from **lakes Ontario and Erie** eastward along the **St. Lawrence River Valley**, nearly halfway to the Gulf of St. Lawrence.

The region was home for many of Canada's earliest permanent French settlers. They traveled inland by boat up the St. Lawrence River and cleared thousands of long and narrow farm lots on both sides of the river. Today, the fertile soil and a growing season of three to four months continue to provide abundant fruits, vegetables, hay, poultry and dairy products. While there are still a large number of small family farms in the region, most of the food produced in the lowlands now comes from huge **mechanized farms**. On these farms, almost all of the work is done by machines operated by only a few farmworkers.

The port at Halifax, Nova Scotia, is free of ice all year long.

The black soil of the flat St. Lawrence Lowlands Region is very fertile because it was once the bottom of an inland sea.

The St. Lawrence/Great Lakes Lowlands Region has become the **manufacturing** and **trade** center of Canada. Transportation equipment, automobiles and parts, iron and steel products of all kinds, cloth and clothing, medicine, high-technology products and industrial and farm chemicals are some of the region's most important products.

The region's success as a manufacturing center is easy to explain. Timber, mineral resources and hydroelectric-power sources are located nearby to the north and west. The region's most important natural waterway, the St. Lawrence River, has been deepened and improved so it can be used by large, ocean-going ships. Airports and super highways also link the region's major cities, many of which are located along the banks of the St. Lawrence River like pearls on a string. Canada's two largest cities and its national capital are located in this region. **Toronto**, Canada's largest city, has a population of nearly four million people. **Montreal** has nearly three million. Canada's capital city, **Ottawa**, is much smaller, but it is the center of the national government.

Skaters and sledders enjoy outdoor winter activities in Montreal, the largest French-speaking city in North America.

THE CANADIAN SHIELD

The **Canadian Shield** is a huge region. Much of it is bare rock, but the shield contains many dense forest areas (in the south) and many thousands of swamps, rivers and lakes. From east to west, the region begins at the edge of the St. Lawrence River Valley and sprawls halfway across the rest of Canada. From south to north, the shield extends from the northern shores of the Great Lakes to surround Hudson Bay and cover most of the Arctic. Some of the oldest rock on earth is found there. The soil that once covered the shield was scraped away by slow moving glaciers many thousands of years ago. Much of it ended up in what today is Ohio, Indiana, Illinois and Michigan.

TOP: A geologist examines a diamond drill core on the Canadian Shield in northern Ontario. Mining is one of the most important economic activities in this barren, but resource-rich, region of Canada.

North of the transcontinental railroad, all-terrain vehicles provide transportation across the Canadian Shield during the summer months.

The shield's rugged and inhospitable landscape forms a 1,000-mile-wide barrier to transportation. For many years, before air transportation, a single pair of railroad tracks across the shield was the only link between eastern and western Canada.

The shield has been both a curse and a blessing for Canadians. Difficult to cross and almost impossible to farm, the region is a storehouse of valuable natural resources and its many rivers provide a vital source of water power. Forestry and mining are its primary industries. Rich deposits of iron ore, copper, nickel, zinc, lead and uranium are found beneath the surface.

During the region's short summers, adventurers willing to endure clouds of vicious blackflies and hungry mosquitoes will find some of the best fishing and hunting in the world in and around the shield's thousands of lakes and rivers.

THE CANADIAN PRAIRIE

The **Prairie Region** of Canada is a flat and fertile area of **plains** and low hills located between the rugged Canadian Shield to the east and north and the Rocky Mountains to the west.

For most of the 20th century, the Prairie Region has been known as Canada's "bread basket." Its millions of acres of wheat and other crops have provided Canadians with most of their bread, cereals and feed grains. In most years, prairie farmers are able to raise a large surplus of grain which is sold to other countries around the world.

Today, the Prairie Region is important for more than its grain. Within the past 50 years, huge reserves of oil and natural gas have been discovered here, bringing new prosperity to western Canada.

Winnipeg, Manitoba, located halfway across Canada and near to the Canada-United States border, sits on the southern edge of the Canadian Shield. Settled in 1812, the city has served as the gateway to western Canada since the railway came in 1885. **Calgary, Alberta**, is located on the western side

The many lakes of the Canadian Shield attract thousands of sport-fishing enthusiasts every year. They use plenty of insect repellant!

Huge machines, called combines, can harvest many acres of grain in a hour. Grain from the Canadian prairies is shipped by rail to ports in British Columbia and the Great Lakes to be sold around the world.

On a spot where grain is harvested, an oil well pumps an even more valuable resource from beneath the earth's surface for a lucky prairie farmer near Calgary, Alberta.

of the Prairie Region. It is one of Canada's fastest growing cities, mainly because of its location close to some of the country's richest fields of oil and natural gas. North of Calgary is Alberta's capital, **Edmonton** which is the largest city in the region.

THE WESTERN MOUNTAINS

The **Western Mountain Region** of Canada is commonly known as "the Rockies." The region extends from the western edge of the prairies to the shores of the Pacific Ocean. Four different mountain ranges are found in this region, with a less rugged **plateau** area located in the middle. All are part of a huge chain of mountains that extends from Alaska to the southern tip of South America.

The soaring peaks of the Rocky Mountains, some of them capped with snow all year long, attract tourists from around the world who come to enjoy the region's crystal lakes and breathtaking scenery.

The **Fraser River** flows southward through the center of the region and almost reaches the Canada-United States border before it turns westward and empties into the Pacific Ocean. The lowland area at the mouth of the river is called the **Fraser Delta**. It is one of the most productive farming areas in Canada and home for 75 percent of the region's three million people.

From the soaring peaks of the Canadian Rockies to the rugged shores of **Vancouver Island**, the region contains some of the most breathtaking scenery in Canada. It is a region of towering waterfalls, crystal lakes, deep chasms and, in the south, dense forests where some of the tallest evergreen trees in the world are found.

The economic activities of the region reflect both its natural resources and its natural beauty. Even though the Rockies contain only 2 percent of Canada's forest land, the region produces 25 percent of the country's forest products. Most are sold to buyers in the United States and Japan. Mining, too, is important. Mineral resources include zinc, lead and coal. The area also contains some of the richest deposits of natural gas in Canada. The protected bays and tiny islands in and around **Vancouver, British Columbia** have helped make that city one of the boating and vacation capitals of the world.

Visitors on horseback travel through a mountain pass in southwestern Alberta.

THE NORTH

The region Canadians call the North is really an extension of the Canadian Shield and the Prairie Region. But its lack of trees and nearly year-long snow and ice set it apart from southern Canada just as surely as any landform. The northern half of the region is a collection of hundreds of islands of varying sizes, closely packed and surrounded by the Arctic and Atlantic oceans. Geographers refer to such an island-packed area as an **archipelago**.

Cold, forbidding and remote, the Arctic North includes almost half of Canada's land mass. For the North's fewer than 50,000 inhabitants, life is

An igloo, constructed with blocks of snow, offers shelter from the bitterly cold temperatures of the North.

a daily struggle for survival. The region's flat, largely treeless landscape—called **tundra**—is almost always frozen. Still, this is a place of magnificent natural beauty and tremendous economic promise. The North is rich in mineral resources that are valuable but hard to reach.

Bone-chilling temperatures, high winds, and a unique condition known as **permafrost** are a constant challenge to both inhabitants and developers. Due to the long periods of freezing temperatures, the ground never completely thaws during the region's extremely short summers. That makes the construction of buildings, roads, railroads and pipelines more difficult and, therefore, more expensive than it is in the southern regions of Canada.

Arctic winters are frigid, with temperatures sometimes dropping to -40° F. Some vehicles must be left running 24 hours a day because if their motors were shut off they would freeze up in minutes. Clothing for this climate is designed to surround the body like a cocoon. Skin exposed to the region's lowest temperatures will freeze in a matter of seconds.

The climate in the far North also limits plant and animal life. Because vegetation is scarce, it takes a huge area of land to provide enough food for even a few hardy creatures. The survival of each living thing depends on the survival of all others. It is no wonder, then, that respect for the land and its creatures, including **caribou**, **polar bear** and **musk ox**, is an important theme in most of the art and folklore of the people who live in this very special region of Canada. ■

Polar bears are one of the wildlife species that inhabit the North. They may look cuddly, but they weigh in at around 800 pounds and, according to writer Andrew Malcolm, can "knock the head off a seal with one swipe." They do their hunting both on land and in the water.

Questions

1. Explain one reason why Canada is so interesting to people who study its geography.

2. What do geographers mean when they say a country has regional diversity?

3. Make a list of the six natural regions of Canada and for each one you list, describe two features of the region.

4. How has the Canadian Shield been both a "curse and a blessing" to the country?

5. WHAT DO YOU THINK? Select one of the natural regions of Canada and describe some of the ways that the region's geography may affect the lives of the people who live there.

CHAPTER 2

Climate and Natural Vegetation

THE FLAG OF CANADA was adopted in 1965. The outside bands on the flag represent the Atlantic and Pacific oceans. The middle band and the maple leaf represent Canada stretching from sea to sea.

TO GUIDE YOUR READING
Look for answers to these questions

1 What explains the extremes and differences in Canada's climate?

2 What factors influence the climate in Canada?

3 What climate types are found in Canada?

4 How does climate affect natural vegetation in the regions of Canada?

5 What is the climate like in the regions where most Canadians live?

INTRODUCTION

Canada's climate, like its geography, is varied and extreme. On a given day, the temperature difference between two locations in the country may be as great as 80° F. Temperatures in some parts of Canada can drop to -40° F during the winter, while in other regions summer temperatures above 90° F are not unusual.

Such extremes are explained by Canada's large size. The factors that affect climate vary greatly from region to region in a country as large as Canada.

Three types of climate are found in Canada: ***arctic***, ***maritime*** *and* ***continental.***

THREE FACTORS INFLUENCE CANADA'S CLIMATE

One factor that affects the climate in every part of Canada is **latitude**; the measure of a location's distance from the equator. During any season and in any part of the world, the farther one travels from the equator, the weaker are the warming rays of the sun. Because Canada's northernmost territories are more than 3,000 miles farther from the equator than regions located near the Canada-United States border, there are great temperature differences between northern and southern Canada.

A second factor influencing Canada's climate is **topography**; surface features such as mountains, plains, plateaus and valleys. Anyone who has seen a snow-peaked mountain in the middle of summer knows that temperatures at high altitudes are cooler than those below. Most of the mountainous region in western Canada rises between 5,000 and 15,000 feet above sea level, a fact that explains its cool temperatures.

These mountain peaks in the Canadian Rockies are so high that the snow on top never melts—not even in the middle of summer.

The oceans that mark the country's eastern and western boundaries, and the interior Great Lakes, are a third influence on Canada's climate. These large bodies of water affect both the temperature and rainfall of nearby land areas. While land heats and cools rapidly as the seasons come and go, water temperatures change more slowly. Inland breezes off the ocean and very large lakes bring cool air to coastal regions during the summer and warm air during the winter.

Ocean breezes also bring moisture. Billions of gallons of water evaporate into the air over oceans and lakes every day. As the moist air drifts over land, the change in temperature causes much of it to condense and fall. The moisture that condenses near the coasts is usually warm enough to fall as rain, even during the winter. Moisture carried higher into the air and farther inland by powerful storms has more time to cool and, during the winter, it often freezes and falls as snow.

THE ARCTIC CLIMATE

The northern half of Canada has an arctic climate. From November to February, the northern third of the Arctic receives only a few hours of daylight. In late December, the sun's rays remain too far south even to peek over the horizon. During the early summer, however, the sun never sets and daylight lasts all night long. It is why the region is often referred to as "the land of the midnight sun".

High noon during winter in the northern Arctic. The sun's rays barely peek over the horizon to cast long shadows on the snow.

The northern two-thirds of the Arctic are treeless. The snow and ice that cover the islands of north eastern Canada, known as the **polar ice caps**, stay frozen all year long. Snow blankets the rest of the Arctic for at least 10 months of the year. In areas where the snow melts during the short summer thaw, the ground is covered with a thin layer of mucky soil, which sits on top of the permafrost. That rich soil rapidly comes alive with millions of fast-growing, tiny plants such as lichens, mosses and a surprising variety of beautiful wildflowers.

Interestingly, because the oceans that border it are frozen during most of the year, the Arctic is actually very dry. Snowfall in most areas measures only a few inches per year, less moisture than falls on the Sahara Desert.

The southern third of the Arctic is often referred to as the **sub-Arctic**. The climate here, while still cold, is less severe than that of the northern two-thirds. There are some trees, which grow very slowly, and the summer growing season is long enough to allow many varieties of brush, grasses and flowers to green the landscape.

During summer, part of the Arctic landscape comes alive with a surprising variety of beautiful wildflowers.

wildlife of the Arctic North

from an original painting by ***Jack Lashway***

Family farms still thrive on tiny Prince Edward Island, thanks to its fertile soil and to the abundant rainfall and long growing season provided by the maritime climate.

THE MARITIME CLIMATE

The areas along the eastern and western coasts of Canada south of the sub-Arctic enjoy a maritime climate. Winter and summer temperatures are less extreme than those farther inland due to the influence of the oceans, whose temperatures change very little from summer to winter. Rainfall on both coasts is abundant, thanks to the flow of moist air that travels across the surface of the ocean waters.

The mild temperatures and abundant rainfall of the maritime climate encourage the growth of natural vegetation. Both coasts are lush and green and covered with dense forests of cedar, spruce and fir. Although the rough terrain and rocky soil found in most coastal areas make large-scale farming difficult, small-scale or family farming is still a way of life for thousands of Canadians on both coasts, thanks to the favorable maritime weather.

The awesome Arctic landscape and the tall green forests of the coastal regions have long been favorite subjects for artists and writers in Canada. An unfortunate result has been to create an image of Canada as a land of dogsleds and lumberjacks.

Most Canadians, however, have made their homes in the many cities located along the country's southern border. They share a continental climate with the millions of Americans who live in the northeastern and midwestern United States.

THE CONTINENTAL CLIMATE

Most of the border area is far removed from the influence of Ocean waters, so its temperatures are more extreme and the air has less moisture. The western interior of Canada is especially dry. The mountains located along the west coast are so wide and so high that little moisture from the Pacific Ocean ever reaches the flat prairie on the other side. Most of the Prairie Region is too dry for trees, but natural grasses and the food grains planted by prairie farmers thrive in the fertile soil.

Continental winters can be very cold. Winter

the wheat that made the prairies grow

It took years of scientific research, sponsored by the Canadian government, to develop a strain of wheat hardy enough to withstand the dry and harsh continental climate of the Canadian prairies. The strain, called Marquis, was developed on an experimental farm in Ottawa in 1903. The first bag of the seed, shipped to Indian Head, Saskatchewan, almost wound up as chicken feed before it could be tested. One of the farmworkers stole it, returning it only after the government official in charge of the experiment posted a sign on the barn that read, "Please, whoever took the sackful of wheat marked Marquis for testing, return it at once. Urgent. No questions asked."

daytime temperatures in Ottawa, for example, seldom rise above freezing and night time temperatures often drop to -10° F. The amount of snowfall in continental regions differs from winter to winter and is very unpredictable. Snowfall is generally greater near the east coast and along the eastern shores of the Great Lakes. In these areas, it is not unusual for residents to awaken on a winter morning to a foot or more of fresh snow.

Much of the snow that falls east of the Great Lakes region is **lake-effect snow**. It is formed when warmer, moist air from above the unfrozen lakes collides with colder air over the land. This occurs most frequently in the late fall and early winter when the lake water is warmest. Residents farther east are affected by huge winter storms which develop just off the east coast of the United States and carry moisture from the Atlantic Ocean hundreds of miles inland. The most powerful of these storms can drop as much as two to three feet of snow on some locations in eastern Canada and the northeastern United States. When they do, the snow clogs highways and slows traffic, forcing work to be delayed and schools to close until the roads can be cleared by huge snowplows.

The people of Quebec have learned to love both their warm summers and cold winters. They stage activities and festivals that take advantage of the extremes of both seasons. OPPOSITE PAGE: This famous ice castle is the central attraction at the Annual Quebec Winter Carnival in Quebec City. LEFT: Face painting is one of many activities connected with the Montreal Jazz Festival held every July. Most concerts are outdoors.

It is no wonder that people living with a continental climate look forward to their hot and sunny summers. July temperatures as far north as Quebec City regularly reach above 80° F during the day as millions of Canadians head for the nearest beach or fire up their barbecues. A frost-free growing season of three to four months provides enough time and usually enough moisture for farmers to grow a variety of vegetable crops and grains.

Natural vegetation also thrives in a continental climate. Across the southern areas of the Canadian Shield and in the St. Lawrence/Great Lakes Lowlands, maple, birch, oak and pine grow thick and tall. During the early autumn, all but the evergreens prepare for winter by shedding their spring growth of leaves. Before falling, however, the leaves lose their green coloring revealing bright shades

Maple trees fill the forests of the St. Lawrence/Great Lakes Lowlands and the southern fringes of the Canadian Shield. In late September and early October, the maple leaves lose their green coloring to turn brilliant hues of orange, yellow and red. The maple leaf was selected as the official symbol of Canada in 1965.

of yellow, red and orange. In early October, the hillsides of southern Canada appear as if on fire as sunshine lights up the brilliant colors of the autumn leaves.

The large number of maple trees in the south central region of Canada, where so many Canadians live, led to the selection of the maple leaf as the country's national symbol. It was an interesting choice. For Canadians living in other parts of the country, including most of the Native peoples, the only maple leaves they ever see are made of red cloth and stitched to their nation's flag. The tree is found almost nowhere else in Canada. ■

Questions

1. What three factors affect the climate in Canada?
2. What three climate types are found in Canada?
3. Why is the Arctic region of Canada so dry?
4. Describe three features of the Canadian Tundra.
5. WHAT DO YOU THINK? How does Canada's climate affect the development of its natural resources?

CHAPTER 3

Using the Land

Most of the fruit eaten in Canada is imported, but the weather in the Okanagan Valley of southern British Columbia is mild enough to support the growth of apples and even grapefruit.

TO GUIDE YOUR READING
Look for answers to these questions

1. How do Canada's geography and climate affect Canadian agriculture?
2. What natural resources are important to the Canadian economy?
3. What products are made by Canadian manufacturers?

INTRODUCTION

Canada has all the ingredients necessary for a prosperous economy. An abundance of many different ***natural resources*** *and a well-educated population have combined to provide Canadians with one of the highest standards of living in the world.*

Though Canadians must depend on other nations for many items they themselves cannot produce, they have many products to offer in trade.

AGRICULTURE

Only 7 percent of Canada's land surface can be used for **agriculture**, but in a country as large as Canada, that is still a lot of land. It is more than enough to provide food for the 29 million people who live there. Because the growing season in most of Canada is so short, however, there are many food products that cannot be grown. Canadians depend on farmers in other countries for, among other things, tropical fruits, white sugar and coffee. During the winter, Canadians depend on farmers in more southern climates for their fresh fruits and vegetables.

Most of Canada's agricultural output comes from the St. Lawrence/Great Lakes Lowlands Region, the southern prairie, eastern coastal regions and the Okanagan Valley, an especially fertile valley in southeastern British Columbia. Elsewhere in Canada, cold weather and rocky terrain combine to make farming either impossible or very difficult.

In Atlantic Canada and in the Western Mountain Region, the terrain is too rugged for large-scale farming. Still, there are thousands of family farms nestled in the many narrow, fertile valleys of both regions. These farms are quite productive, despite their size, thanks to the maritime climate, which provides abundant rainfall and a growing season of more than four months. Instead of specializing in one product, most of these small farms produce a variety of dairy foods, meat, poultry and vegetables, for local markets.

Prince Edward Island, the smallest province, produces nearly one-third of Canada's potatoes every year.

By contrast, agriculture in the St. Lawrence/Great Lakes Lowlands region is dominated by huge farms that use the most up-to-date farm machinery and which specialize in only a few products. Some of these mechanized farms, called **factory farms**, are owned by companies that sell huge quantities of products to grocery stores and fast-food chains across Canada and the United States. The most common factory farm products are chicken, beef, pork, eggs and potatoes.

During late summer, wooden stands in the Byward Market in downtown Ottawa overflow with the abundant farm harvest of the fertile St. Lawrence and Ottawa river valleys.

Many family farms remain in this region, but, like small farmers in the United States, small farmers in Canada have a difficult time competing with the factory farms. One result has been a decrease in the number of farmers in both countries. In 1900, more than half of all Canadians lived and worked on farms. Today, fewer than 4 percent of Canadians are farmers.

Whatever their size, the farms of the St. Lawrence/Great Lakes Lowlands Region produce a wide array of fruits and vegetables. Their growing season begins in early May and often lasts until the final days of September. A late summer walk through the Byward Market, only a few steps from the Parliament Buildings in downtown Ottawa, provides a dazzling display of the region's bountiful harvest: lettuce, cabbage, tomatoes, colorful peppers, carrots, radishes, onions, potatoes, corn, squash, apples, blueberries and—just in time for Halloween—huge orange pumpkins.

Further west, on the other side of the Canadian Shield, prairie farmers make an important contribution to the nation's grocery basket and to the world's food supply with bumper harvests of wheat, barley, oats, flax, sunflowers and other seed grains. The Prairie Region has almost always supplied more grain than Canadians themselves can consume. Much of each year's harvest is stored in the many brightly painted grain elevators that dot the prairie landscape along the railways. The grain is shipped across Canada and around the world all year long.

Fishing for herring off the coast of New Brunswick. Schools of the fish are fenced in by poled netting, which forms a weir. The flock of seagulls is a sign that the fishing boat is in the right spot.

FISHING CANADIAN WATERS

In the first light of morning, fishing boats along both coasts of Canada make their way out of protected ports and head for the open seas. Nets are set and lines are cast as their owners watch for the day's first catch.

With more than 18,000 miles of ocean coastline and nearly 20 percent of the world's fresh water, it is not surprising that Canada is one of the world's leading suppliers of fish and producers of fish products. The vast number of fish found in the waters of Newfoundland's Grand Banks was a major reason why both France and England were so anxious to establish a presence in Canada centuries ago.

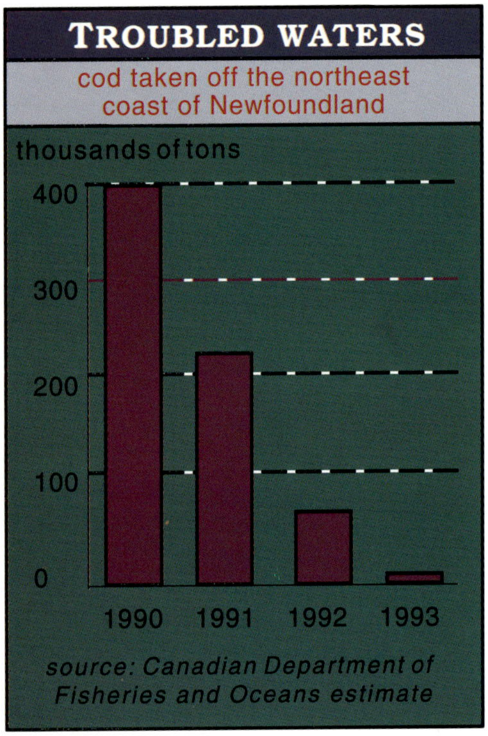

The waters along Canada's southeast coast are still alive with fish, but their numbers are declining at an alarming rate because of overfishing, a lot of it done by fishing vessels from other countries. Until recently, more than a billion pounds of cod, haddock, halibut and other varieties were pulled from the cool North Atlantic every year. In 1992 and again in 1994, the Canadian government placed strict limits on the number of fish that could be taken from the waters of Atlantic Canada. Some parts of the Atlantic were declared off limits for fishing until further notice in the hope that the fish would breed and recover their numbers. But, some scientists fear that fishing in the North Atlantic will never be the same again. Closer to shore, though, lobster, herring and oysters are still plentiful in the shallow waters along the shores of the Gulf of St. Lawrence, the Bay of Fundy, Prince Edward Island and Newfoundland.

This photo of fishing boats at low tide in New Brunswick captures the somber mood of this once thriving industry. After providing an enjoyable and prosperous way of life for many generations of Canadians living along the Atlantic coast, the industry hit bottom during the early 1990s. With the number of fish declining at an alarming rate due to overfishing, the Canadian government placed heavy restrictions on the yearly catch, hoping that the stocks would rebuild over time.

Lobster traps are checked every morning starting at the crack of dawn. By noon, the tasty crustaceans are being enjoyed at lunch in restaurants up and down the coast, or readied for shipment to buyers across Canada and the United States.

Shucking scallops. Wearing protective gloves, the shucker uses one tool both to open the shell and to pop out each sweet and tender scallop.

Another of Canada's fishing grounds is located just off the country's west coast. Here, much of the world's salmon is caught and readied for market. These Pacific waters also yield large catches of halibut, herring, tuna and a number of lesser-known species. Preparing the fish for shipment to grocery stores across Canada and around the world creates thousands of jobs for Canadians in the processing, canning and packaging industries.

There are thousands of large and small lakes in the interior, most of which are filled with a range of delicious freshwater species. These provide valuable income for people who fish for a living. The lakes are also major attractions for many people from all over North America who come to Canada to enjoy some of the most exciting freshwater fishing in the world.

Half of Canada's total fish exports are purchased by people in the United States, who spend nearly a billion dollars a year on Candian fish and fish products.

Salmon fishing on Canada's Pacific coast provides thousands of jobs in the processing, canning and packaging industries.

LUMBERING AND MINING

Canada is the world's leading producer of newsprint. Most of it is used for newspapers in the United States.

The forestry industry puts tens of thousands of Canadians to work from coast to coast in logging, forest management, and in the manufacturing and transporting of wood products.

Nearly 40 percent of Canada's total land area is covered by forest; almost all of it is in the southern half of the country. Canadian manufacturers take advantage of the country's wealth of forest resources to produce millions of dollars worth of wood products including building materials, furniture, paper and paper products. Canada is, for example, the world's leading producer of newsprint, three-quarters of which is purchased by publishers in the United States. Also, millions of Christmas trees purchased by Canadians and Americans each December come from the dense forests that form the southern boundary of the Canadian Shield.

Lumbering has been an important industry in Canada since before the country was born. Gasoline-powered chainsaws and trucks (above) have replaced handsaws and horse-drawn sleighs (below), but taking wood from the forest is still hard work.

Tiiiim-berrrrrr....

Researchers are developing a way to control robotic mining vehicles that can work thousands of feet underground while being controlled by an operator working on the surface.

An underground miner in Thompson, Manitoba. Canada produces a greater quantity and a larger variety of minerals than any other country.

Crunchhhhh

Even more wealth lies underground. Canada produces more nickel than any other country. It is also among the world's leading producers of such minerals as silver, zinc, cobalt, uranium, gypsum, gold, copper, lead and asbestos.

Canada is the world's premier exporter of fossil fuels. The most important of these are coal, natural gas and oil. More than 90 percent of the production of these three resources takes place in western Canada. No one really knows how much more lies beneath the permafrost of the Arctic, but most experts believe it to be a lot. The Prairie Region of Canada is known to contain more than three times as much oil as all of the Arab states together. Unfortunately, most of it is difficult and expensive to extract.

The oil that lies beneath the frozen surface of the north, for example, is a long way from the places where it would be sold and ground transportation across the region is extremely difficult. The permafrost makes railroad construction all but impossible. The tracks would sink into the muck during the first thaw.

1

Drilling rigs pump oil from pools found hundreds of feet below the earth's surface. In Canada, oil is taken from three major locations: southern Alberta and the ocean floor just off the coasts of both the Atlantic and Arctic Oceans. Offshore drilling takes place from floating rigs. Wherever they drill, oil companies must work with great care in order to avoid spills that would damage the environment.

2

Pipelines, many of them hundreds of miles long, carry oil from the drill sites to huge refineries located near Canada's major cities. Only some of the pipelines are buried beneath the ground. Special bridges are built over the above-ground lines so the pipe will not interfere with the migratory habits of wildlife in their seasonal quest for food.

3

To *refine* means to *purify* or *improve*. Refineries purify crude oil and process it to create a variety of products such as home heating oil, kerosene and gasoline. These refineries are carefully managed to prevent spills, explosions or dangerous fumes from damaging the environment.

PRODUCTION

Turning raw materials into finished products for sale

THESE PICTURES SHOW the steps that are necessary to produce gasoline. From raw material to finished product, much work is involved before oil from beneath the earth's surface finds its way to the pump at your local service station.

4

Petroleum products from the refineries are transported in tanks carried by railroad cars and trucks to the places they will be sold.

5

Stored in huge underground tanks, the gasoline is sold at service stations across Canada and in the United States.

Beaufort Sea
Alaska (United States)
OIL
(off-shore)
Great Bear Lake
HUNTING & TRAPPING
Pacific Ocean
Great Slave Lake
FISHING
WOOD
& PAPER
PRODUCTS
Lake Athabasca
OIL &
NATURAL GAS
Lake Winnipeg
AGRICULTURE
500 km
0
500 Miles

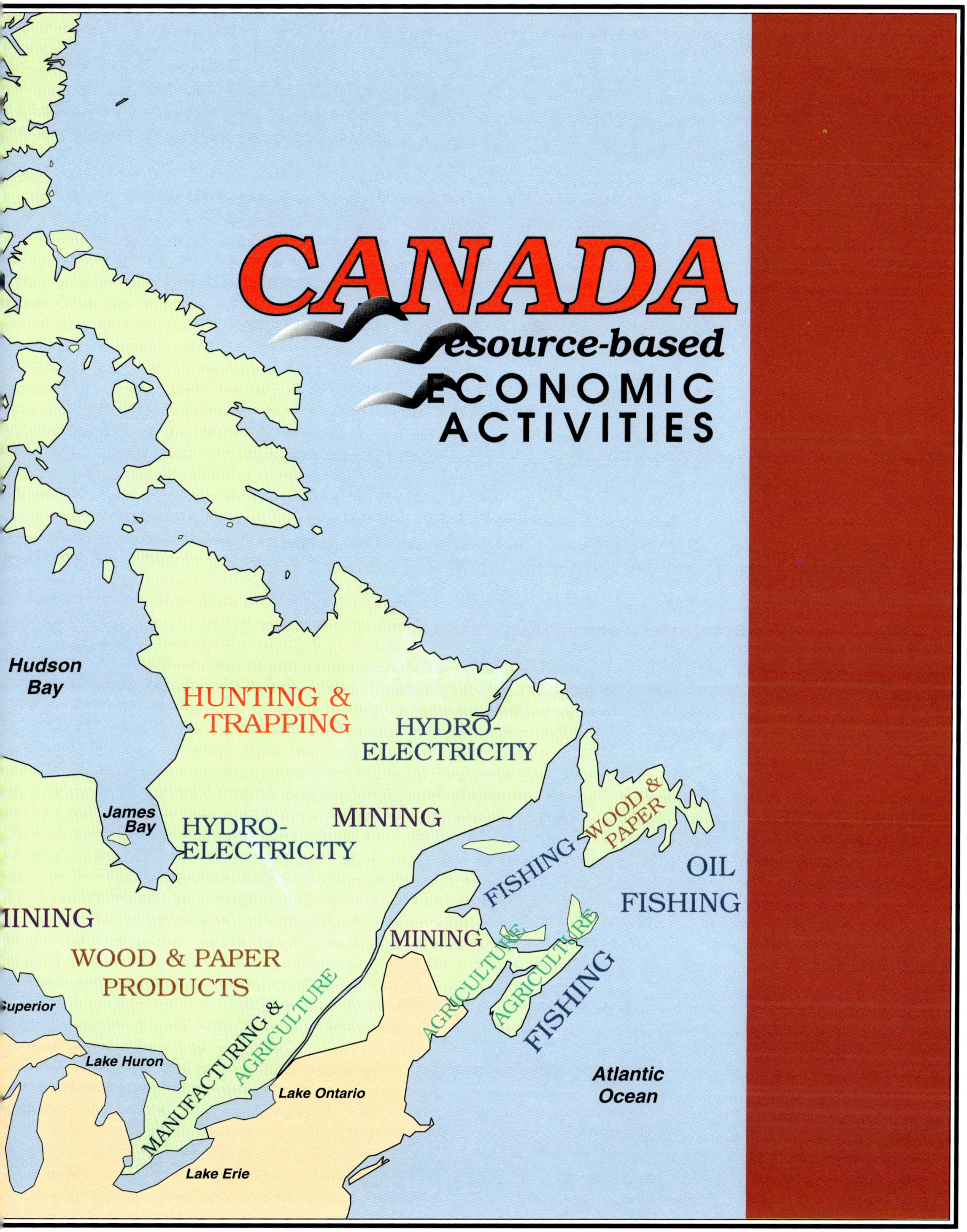
CANADA
Resource-based
ECONOMIC
ACTIVITIES
Hudson Bay
HUNTING & TRAPPING
HYDRO-ELECTRICITY
James Bay
HYDRO-ELECTRICITY
MINING
WOOD & PAPER
FISHING
OIL
FISHING
MINING
MINING
WOOD & PAPER PRODUCTS
AGRICULTURE
AGRICULTURE
AGRICULTURE
FISHING
Superior
MANUFACTURING & AGRICULTURE
Lake Huron
Lake Ontario
Atlantic Ocean
Lake Erie

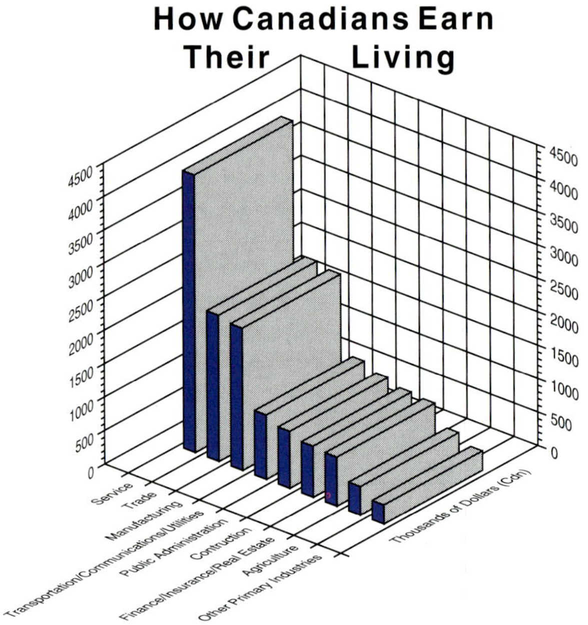

Only a small portion of the oil found beneath the prairies can easily be tapped by drilling rigs like those used in Texas and Oklahoma. Instead of being found in pools between the layers of rock that make up the earth's crust, most of the oil in western Canada is found near the surface, soaked into the soil. The oil in these so-called **tar sands** can be extracted, but the process is slow and expensive. As the nations of the world use up the supplies of easy-to-obtain oil, however, Canada's huge reserves may become more and more vital.

MANUFACTURING

The power of many of Canada's long, swiftly moving rivers has been harnessed to provide the power to spin huge electricity-producing machines called **turbines**. More than half of the country's electricity is generated this way. The process is called **hydroelectric production**. A growing amount of Canada's hydroelectric power travels through thousands of miles of thick cables to light, heat or cool millions of homes in the United States.

Building a turbine at a new hydroelectric project in northern Quebec.

At hydroelectric system control centers, decisions about power generation, transmission and sharing power with other systems are made around the clock.

Canada's abundance of raw materials and energy resources has helped it become one of the world's leading industrial nations. In fact, manufacturing is the country's single most important economic activity. Each year, Canadian factories manufacture billions of dollars worth of transportation vehicles and parts, machinery, chemicals, paper products, electrical equipment, wood products, processed food and much more. Most are produced by companies that have factories and do business in both Canada and the United States.

TOURISM

Renowned for its scenery, outdoor activities and European flavor, Canada is a favorite destination for vacationers from around the world. Montreal, Quebec City, Vancouver and Toronto are especially popular for world travelers eager to sample a different culture, to see great art, to attend concerts, enjoy live theater and museum displays and to watch professional sporting events.

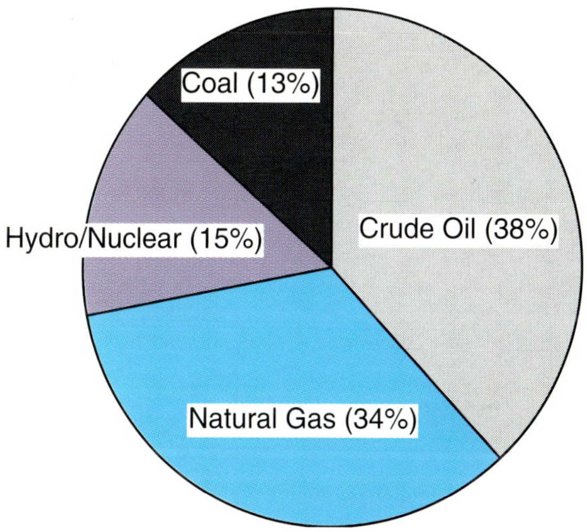

Where Canada's Energy Comes From

Others are attracted by Canada's vast wilderness and the opportunity it offers to "get away from it all." They come to catch five-pound bass and yard-long northern pike, to hunt black bear and caribou or to view some of the most spectacular scenery in the world.

From the manicured golf courses of Prince Edward Island to the rugged wilderness of the Yukon, Canada is a world-renowned destination for tourists and outdoor-sports enthusiasts.

The Canadian tourism industry is a source of jobs for hundreds of thousands of hotel, motel, resort and restaurant employees, hunting and fishing guides, ski instructors and souvenir-makers. ■

The French culture and delicious food found in Quebec attract international visitors.

Questions

1. Where are most of Canada's farms located?
2. What are factory farms?
3. Why is Canada's fishing industry so important to people living in the United States?
4. What jobs are created by Canada's huge forests?
5. WHAT DO YOU THINK? In what ways are the natural resources of Canada important to the United States?

UNIT 2

the history of Canada

A CHILD OF WARRING PARENTS

The character of a nation is shaped not only by its geography but also by its history.

Modern Canada is the child of warring parents, England and France, both of which left their marks on Canada's culture and on its soul. For more than 150 years, settlers and soldiers from these two European nations struggled to take control of North America, first from the continent's Native peoples and then from each other. Though England won the struggle, the language and culture of the Native peoples and French Canadians have remained very much alive.

Canada's history from the time the English took control is a story of conflict and compromise among the country's founding peoples that continue to this day.

ESSAY

Native peoples, Founding peoples

With their imposing ships anchored downriver, French explorer Jacques Cartier and his men cruise up the St. Lawrence as startled North Americans look on, not knowing quite what to make of these strange-looking visitors and their even stranger-looking sailing vessels. This was the first of many fateful meetings between Native Americans and Europeans. Neither group would ever be the same.

Hoping to find a water route to Asia, where they would trade for spices and silk, European sailors spent most of the 16th century poking the noses of their tiny wooden ships into every inlet they could find along the east coast of North America in search of a way through the continent.

Disappointed with their lack of success, the explorers soon discovered that North America was much bigger and far more interesting than they had earlier imagined. It seemed as though every expedition crew found a new natural treasure: coastal waters teeming with fish and whales; tall, thick forests filled with wildlife and, most importantly, land as far as the eye could see. So while their search for a passage to Asia continued, the Europeans began laying claim to as much of North America as they could explore and settle.

The continent, however, was already occupied by hundreds of thousands of Native peoples whose ancestors had lived there for many thousands of years. Most were willing and friendly trade partners with the earliest visitors. But conflict developed when groups of European settlers began setting up permanent homes and villages in North America as if they owned the continent.

The differences in culture between the Native peoples of North America and the European visitors went far deeper than language and clothing. Each group had very different ideas about the land. To the Europeans, land was something to claim, to own and to defend. Developing a piece of land added to its value, and the owner could then sell the property for profit. To most of the Native peoples, the land was to be shared and carefully maintained for future generations. As their only source of life, the land and its wildlife were treated with great respect and also played central roles in many of their religions.

No one will ever be able to prove whether it would have made any difference if the Europeans had had a better understanding of native cultures. But, because no boundary lines or property deeds existed, it is clear that the Europeans felt that land in North America was there for the taking. Greatly overpowered by European weapons, there was little the Native peoples could do about it. As their numbers grew, the Europeans drew boundaries and later created countries where none had ever existed before. North America and the lives of its Native population, virtually unchanged for 15,000 years, would never be the same. ■

Native leader Sa Ga Yeath Qua Pieth Tow posed for this formal portrait in 1710.

CHAPTER 4

The Struggle for Control of a Continent

1500-1763

Native North Americans taught the Europeans some vital skills. During their first winter in North America in 1535, many of Jacques Cartier's men became ill with scurvy. The people of the St. Lawrence Valley shared their cure: tea brewed from spruce bark.

TO GUIDE YOUR READING
Look for answers to these questions

1. Why did both France and England establish colonies in North America during the 1600s and 1700s?
2. Why did so few people settle in New France as compared to the number of people who made their homes in the English colonies?
3. How did English and French rivalries in North America affect the lives of the continent's Native peoples?
4. How did England gain control of North America?

INTRODUCTION

The discovery of North America by European explorers gave England and France, longtime rivals for power in Europe, a new source of conflict. Their struggle for control of the continent, which began in the early 1600s, lasted for more than 150 years.

Each nation had different ideas about what it hoped to gain by controlling North America, although both wanted greater wealth and power. England, much smaller in size than France, was more interested in claiming land for settlement. The land would have to be taken by force from the Native peoples who had lived on it for generations. France had plenty of land at home, but the riches of North America, especially fish and furs, were too tempting to pass up.

THE FRENCH STAKE THEIR CLAIMS

French claims in North America were based on the voyages of **Jacques Cartier**, who made three trips up the **St. Lawrence River** during the mid-1500s. Cartier had been hired by the king of France to find a water route through the continent and perhaps some gold and silver along the way. He found neither.

Although he reported having friendly encounters with the Native people living along the St. Lawrence River, Cartier returned home unimpressed with most of what he had found in North America. During one of his voyages along the shores of **Newfoundland**, he wrote in his diary,

this land should not be called New Land, being composed of stones and horrible rugged rocks. . . . I did not see one cartload of earth and yet I landed at many places. . . . there is nothing but moss and short stunted shrub.

Cartier's lack of success discouraged the French from attempting to found permanent settlements in North America for the rest of that century. Still, French sailors returned often to fish the Grand Banks off the coast of Newfoundland and to buy furs from the Native peoples who lived near the Gulf of St. Lawrence. Especially prized were the pelts of the North American beaver.

Jacques Cartier plants a cross on Canadian soil in 1534. Sensing that Cartier and his men were laying claim to their land, Native leader Donnacona was enraged. He angrily informed the French visitors that his people had lived in this place forever.

When felt hats made from beaver fur became popular in Europe during the 1500s, the value of the pelts soared. By the end of the century, competition in the North American fur trade was fierce. Hoping to profit from furs, the king of France convinced the explorer **Samuel de Champlain** to establish a permanent French presence in North America. In 1605, Champlain established the first French settlement at **Port Royal**, located on the eastern shore of the Bay of Fundy. The tiny colony that developed there was named **Acadia**.

THE STRUGGLE BEGINS IN THE GULF OF ST. LAWRENCE

After a rocky start, Acadia thrived, thanks to excellent fishing and fertile soil. Unfortunately, Acadia turned out to be a dangerous place to live. The Acadians were under constant threat of attack by English gunboats which were trying to scare them away. Acadia's location near the gulf of the St. Lawrence River was at the doorway to the most direct route from Europe to the interior of North America. Whoever controlled Acadia controlled access to the profitable fur trade and to whatever riches might later be discovered.

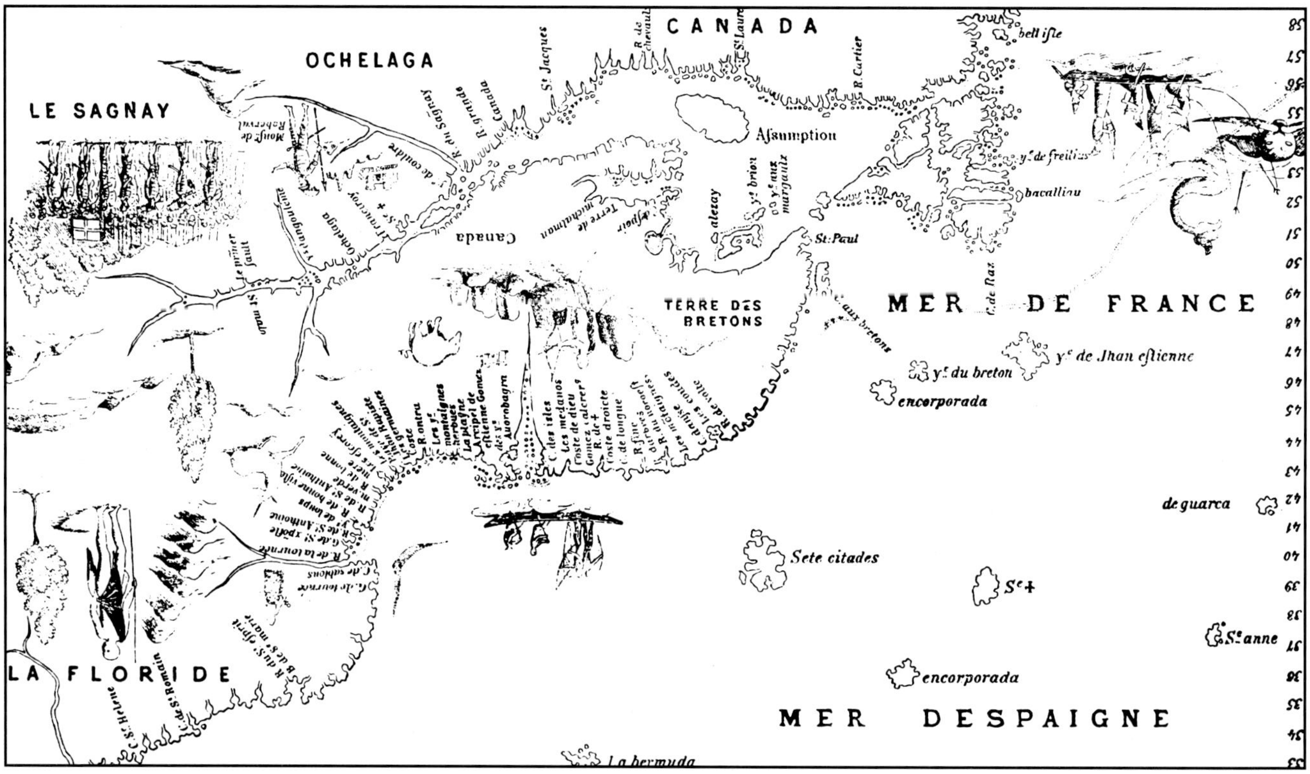

An early map of Canada, drawn sometime around 1543, shows the considerable discoveries of the explorer Jacques Cartier.

Busy with problems at home, the French king did little to protect his interests in Acadia. Largely ignored, the Acadians developed a friendly and flourishing trade relationship with the wealthy British colonies farther down the coast.

Samuel de Champlain trades with the Native people of the St. Lawrence Valley in the early 1600s. European explorers brought more than trinkets and iron knives to North America. Rats, never before seen on the continent, escaped from the ships and soon spread across the land. Seeds carried on the boots of sailors introduced many new forms of vegetation to the continent—including dandelions. The most unwelcome imports were measles, small pox, tuberculosis and other diseases unknown to Native North Americans. With no immunity from unfamiliar viruses and bacteria, the Native population was ravaged by terrible epidemics. Nearly 90 percent of the people died, and whole nations disappeared as a result.

ESTABLISHING NEW FRANCE

England and France were soon fighting over who would control the fur trade and fishing in North America. Three years after Acadia was settled, Champlain helped establish a second French colony farther inland on the shores of the St. Lawrence River at **Quebec**.

Champlain dreamed of turning his tiny settlement into a prosperous Catholic colony in the St. Lawrence Valley, but that dream was never realized during his lifetime. Only a few people were willing to put up with the region's long and frigid winters, especially when it took only a year's work in the fur trade to earn them enough money to live comfortably at home in Europe.

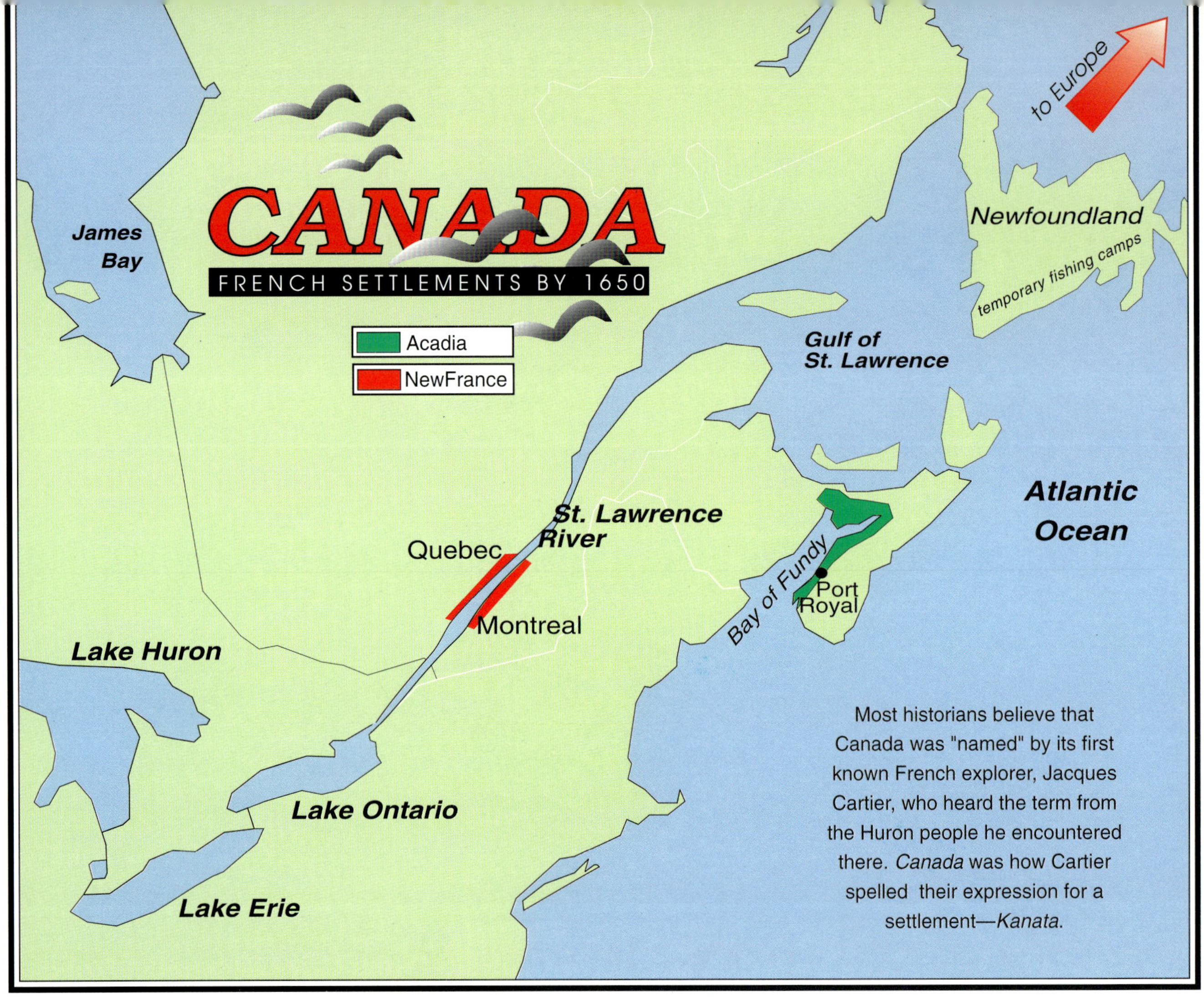

Also, until 1663, French claims in New France were ruled by a handful of businessmen interested only in personal profits. For many years, they discouraged people from setting up farms in the region, fearing that land-clearing settlers might destroy the natural habitat of the beaver and hurt their business. Partly because of this policy, early New France developed a very different character from that of the English colonies to the south.

While English settlers along the Atlantic coast cleared land and rooted themselves in their communities, the French instead were on the move. Traveling in sturdy canoes, they plunged deep into the heartland of the continent in pursuit of the furbearing beaver and other animals. Catholic priests came from France to bring Christianity to the native peoples and to maintain the religious life of the region's few settlers. Thus the character of New France took root in its rivers, furs, and Catholic religion.

An early map of New France.

Although the territory explored and claimed for France by its fur traders was huge, for most of its first century New France remained little more than a collection of forts and trading posts with a tiny population of wandering fur traders and priests.

THE FUR TRADE LEADS TO CONFLICT IN THE INTERIOR

During the first half of the 1600s, the North American fur trade was centered on two regions, each controlled by a different tribe of Native peoples. French traders dealt with the **Huron** who lived and trapped in the region north and west of the St. Lawrence River. A few hundred miles to the south, Dutch traders conducted a thriving business in the Mohawk and Hudson river valleys with the **Iroquois** people. The area, in what is today New York State, had been claimed for the Dutch by Henry Hudson in 1609. The Huron and the Iroquois had been bitter enemies since the Europeans arrived. Their competition in the fur trade only made matters worse.

Faced with a decrease in the beaver population in their territory by the middle of the 1600s, Iroquois trappers headed north into Huron territory. England became involved in the developing conflict when its king, Charles II, seized the Dutch claims in North America. As soon as England joined forces with the Iroquois in the fur trade, the conflict between Britain and France became much more dangerous.

A fur-trade market in Montreal. In the early years, Native people were not allowed inside the gates of the fortified trading posts.

THE RACE FOR MORE TERRITORY

To avoid contact with the Iroquois, many French fur traders headed west. By 1648, two of them, Pierre Radisson and Médard Chouart, Sieur des Groseilliers, had paddled all the way to Lake Superior. They later carried their trade as far north as Hudson Bay. The pair found that it was easier to ship their furs directly to Europe by way of Hudson Bay and so became the first French traders to bypass the Montreal merchants. The practice got them in hot water with the governor of New France, who fined them for trading without a permit. In angry response, the two set sail for London to see if the king of England might be more interested in their discoveries in the fur-rich Hudson Bay region. He was, and sponsored a return voyage by Radisson and des Groseilliers. This resulted in the establishment of the **Hudson's Bay Company** in 1670. France's missed opportunity turned out to be a major victory for England in the struggle for North America. The company grew and soon controlled the entire fur trade north and northwest of the Great Lakes. It maintained this powerful position for the next two centuries.

French prospects improved when **Louis Jolliet** and **Father Jacques Marquette** found their way to the Mississippi River in 1673 and traveled nearly half of its length. Nine years later, René-Robert Cavelier, the **Sieur de la Salle** sailed down river to the Gulf of Mexico in 1682. La Salle claimed the

Mississippi River and much of the surrounding land for France. He named the region **Louisiana** after the French king, Louis XIV. By the end of the century, French forts and trading posts were scattered across the region of the Great Lakes and along the Mississippi all the way to New Orleans.

Voyageurs shooting the rapids. Most of their canoes were made of birch bark.

A French fur trader strikes a deal with a Native North American family.

The unhappy marriage of Hélène de Champlain

IN 1610, during one of his winter visits to France, Samuel de Champlain decided it was time for him to marry. The explorer was in his mid-40s by then and still a bachelor. His search for a wife led him to Nicolas Boullé, a member of the King's court. After some negotiation, it was agreed that Champlain would marry Boullé's daughter, Hélène. She was not yet 12 years old.

They were married on December 30 and celebrated by touring the sights of Paris and enjoying the pleasures of the King's court. According to an agreement between Champlain and Monsieur Boullé, the new couple would not actually live together until Hélène reached her 14 th birthday. Their two-month honeymoon ended in February when Samuel set sail for Quebec without her to get a head start on the competition for the coming fur-trading season.

Returning to France in the fall, Champlain was seriously injured before making it home to Paris. The horse he was riding stumbled, tossing him to the ground and then falling on top of him. Champlain was unable to leave the roadside inn where he had been taken after the accident until early spring. Young Hélène's marriage was off to a rocky start. Their first reunion, however, was a happy one. Champlain presented his wife with two gifts he had brought from Quebec: beaded moccasins and a sweetgrass basket decorated with porcupine quills.

Still, while Champlain was a talented, sensitive and brave man, he was not much of a husband. After spending just a few weeks with Hélène, he once again returned to Quebec. He spent only a few winters with his wife during the first 10 years of their marriage. In 1620, Champlain finally asked the now 22-year old Hélène to join him in Quebec to live. By now a very pampered young lady, accustomed to comfortable surroundings and fine dining, Hélène was horrified at what she found waiting for her on the banks of the St.

Lawrence River. The Habitation, which was to be their home, had been abandoned and was in a terrible state, mainly due to a badly leaking roof. No amount of repair work or fine silks or fancy, imported furniture could change the fact that life in early New France was primitive and very lonely. Hélène was miserable. After four years, the couple packed up and returned to France.

Champlain's Habitation at Quebec as it looked in 1608. It no doubt appeared less inviting during the spring of 1620 when Champlain brought his wife Hélène there to live. Years of neglect and a leaky roof had taken their toll. After spending an unhappy four years trying to make a go of it, the couple packed their belongings and headed home to France. Hélène never set foot in the place again.

After a year spent trying to mend their relationship, Samuel and Hélène finally gave up and Samuel moved back to Quebec. They remained separated until 1629 when Champlain returned to press the King for greater support of New France and to finish writing the last of his many fascinating books. In 1633, he returned to his beloved but struggling colony. Hélène never saw her husband again. He died on Christmas day, 1635, just five days before what would have been the couple's 25th wedding anniversary.

THE VOYAGEURS (travelers) of New France were some of the most colorful characters in Canadian history. They traveled winter and summer throughout the northern half of North America as the water dogs of the fur trade, withstanding incredible hardships while trying to survive in the wild. The voyageurs were the backbone of the French colonial economy. Their search for new sources of furs pushed the boundaries of New France south and west of the Great Lakes and northward across much of the Canadian Shield.

Voyageurs of the Hudson's Bay Company begin their annual expedition. They sometimes had to walk in order to avoid dangerous rapids or to change rivers, carrying canoes and heavy packs on their backs.

The fur companies preferred their voyageurs to be small in stature. Cargo space was too valuable to be taken up by oversized men. But, whatever they may have lacked in height, they made up for in muscle, building huge shoulders and arms by paddling 16 to 18 hours a day for weeks at a time.

To bypass dangerous rapids or to get from one river to another, the voyageurs sometimes had to travel by foot. These overland jaunts, called portages, were sometimes as long as 10 miles over rough terrain. Canoes and supply packs weighing up to 90 pounds each had to be carried through the often thick forest.

As adventurous as the job could be—it involved camping under the stars, spotting new forms of wildlife, meeting fascinating native peoples—the voyageurs often suffered through periods of boredom and exhaustion. Many nights they paddled until dawn without ever putting to shore. When they did sleep, it was usually for only five or six hours on ground that was, more often than not, hard and cold. What time they had to relax was usually spent with their canoes, racing and shooting the rapids.

Their favorite snack was pemmican. This was a mixture of dried and pounded meat, usually buffalo, bear or deer, which was mixed with berries and held together with grease. Those who made pemmican at supply camps were often careless.

It was not unusual to discover hair, leaves, sand, bugs, sticks or other such items in the mixture. But this tasty food stored well and was easy to carry. It was eaten dry or sometimes mixed with water, flour and sugar to form a soup called rubbaboo. The voyageurs also ate meat and fish when they could. Occasionally, they ran across eggs in the wild. But the cook had to be careful because the eggs of turtles (which are good to eat) and those of rattlesnakes (which, of course, are not) look a lot alike. Even for a hardened voyageur, it must have been an unpleasant surprise to discover that the "black hair" found in a breakfast egg treat was actually a baby snake!

the voyageurs Could YOu CuT iT ?

The voyageur's clothing was as distinctive as that of any lumberjack or sailor. He wore the same items summer and winter: red wool cap, short shirt, deer skin leggings, breech cloth and deerskin moccasins with no socks. The outfit was topped off by a bright sash worn with a small pouch. Frequently, bright plumes were also part of the outfit.

However exciting, the life of a voyageur was usually a short one. Few ever saw their 30th birthday. Starvation, hernia, infection, drowning, exposure, rabies and scurvy were only some of the fatal occupational hazards. For doing this brutally hard work and accepting its many risks, the voyageurs were paid about 100 dollars a year.

Adapted from a paper by Ruth Writer, Buchanan High School, Buchanan Michigan.

These two paintings demonstrate the tremendous size of the territory in North America explored and claimed by both the English and French by the end of the 1600s. RIGHT: Traders on Hudson's Bay Company ships barter with an Inuit hunter near the Upper Savage Islands in the Hudson Straight, Northwest Territories.

The Sieur de la Salle sails down the Mississippi River headed for the Gulf of Mexico.

THE NATIVE PEOPLES ARE CAUGHT IN THE MIDDLE

To protect their claims in the Louisiana territory, the French joined with the Native peoples in trying to hold back the growing stream of English colonists making their way west across the Appalachian Mountains. Most of the Native peoples, caught in the middle of a struggle between two European nations for control of their own land, sided with the French. The French traders spent much of their time living among the Native peoples, sharing in their culture and often marrying Native women. They were seen as visitors who paid for what they took home—unlike the growing number of settlers from England and other European countries who considered the Native population a nuisance to be pushed aside in the quest for land.

By 1750, French claims and English settlers had bumped against one another in the **Ohio River Valley** between the Appalachian Mountains and the Mississippi River. English attempts to settle the region were met with armed resistance by the Native peoples and their French allies. Within five years, both England and France were sending reinforcements to North America. The time had come to settle the conflict once and for all.

THE FRENCH ACADIANS ARE FORCED FROM THEIR HOMES

After losing one of its many wars with England, France surrendered Acadia in 1713. England changed the name of its new colony to **Nova Scotia.** In 1755, with another war against France brewing, the English governor of Nova Scotia required French-speaking Acadians still living to take an oath of loyalty to England. Those who refused were ordered to leave. As a result, hundreds of French families, nearly 8,000 people in all, were forced from their homes and herded like cattle aboard English ships. Many died at sea. Some were dropped off in the New England colonies and other

The French and English frontiers, 1700–1763. This hand-drawn map appeared in a popular history book written for Canadian students earlier in this century.

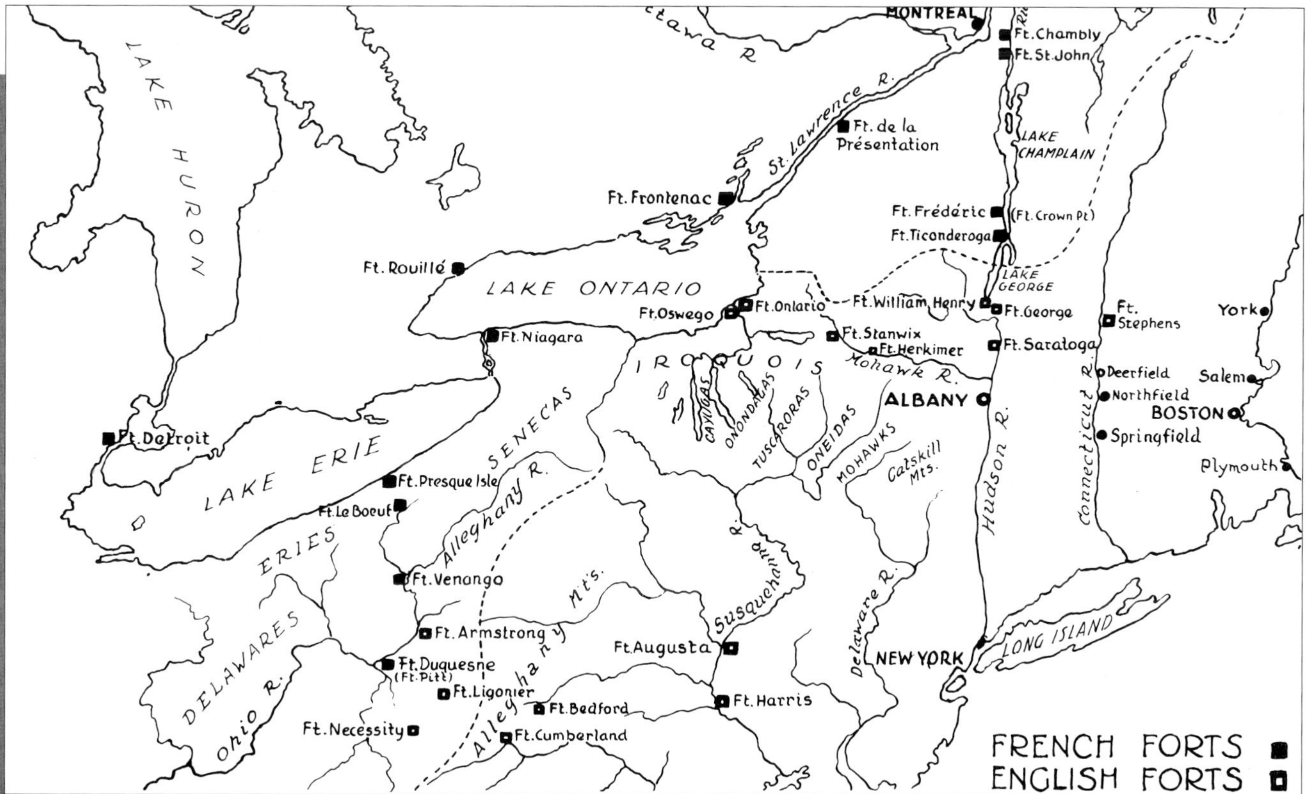

Under the watchful eyes of British troops, Acadian families begin the painful forced departure from their homeland in1755.

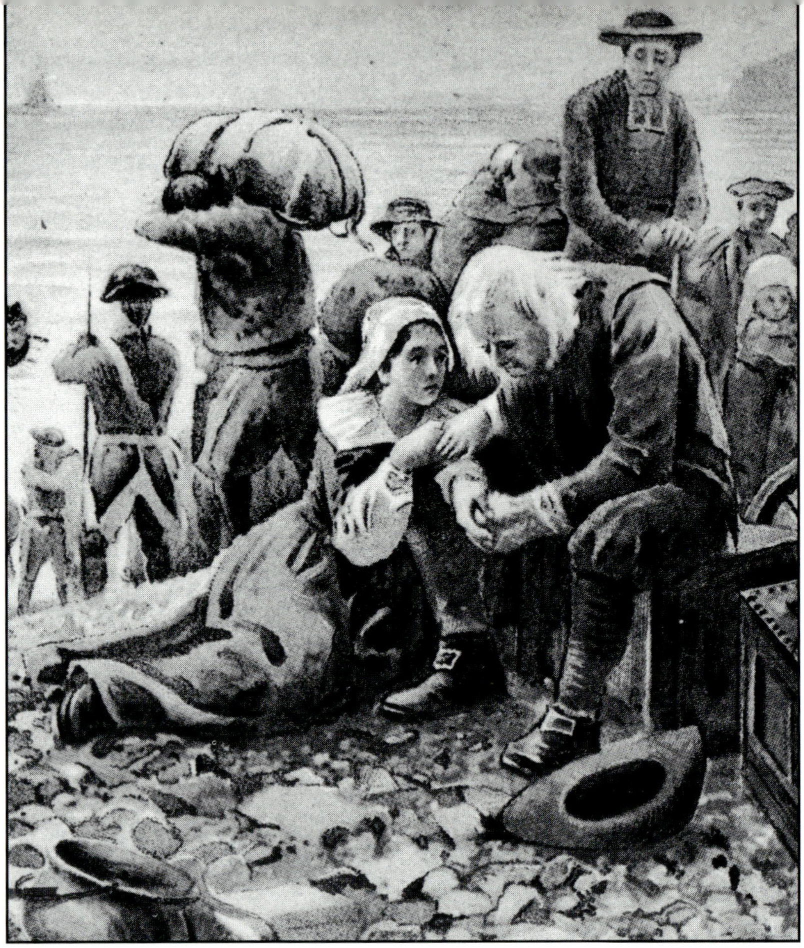

EVANGELINE

THE TRAGIC EXPULSION of the Acadians provided inspiration for one of America's most treasured poems, Henry Wadsworth Longfellow's story of *Evangeline*, (1847). Longfellow was one of America's greatest writers. In the poem, 17-year-old Evangeline is separated from her boyfriend in the confusion of the deportation. They are reunited only near the end of their lives and Evangeline's long lost love, now a very old man, dies in her arms. Some say that Longfellow based his work on a story he had been told by a preacher friend in Boston about a real woman named Evangeline Bellefontaine. The preacher learned of the sad tale from one of his church members who had relatives in Nova Scotia, where the Acadians lived.

colonies to the south, where their descendants continue to be proud of their Acadian heritage. Others wound up in the Louisiana territory, where the Acadian influence is still obvious. The largest community developed near what is today the city of New Orleans, Louisana where the term *Acadian*, spoken too fast, came out *'cajun*. **Cajun** culture has helped to shape the unique character of New Orleans.

THE ENGLISH TAKE CONTROL

In 1756, the last of the Acadians in Nova Scotia were being rounded up when yet another war between England and France broke out in Europe. It soon spread to North America. The **Seven Years' War**, or the **French and Indian War**, as it was called by the British colonists, was the final chapter in a century-long rivalry between the two countries.

Although the French claimed a number of early victories, their prospects in North America faded quickly. One by one, French forts and trading posts along the Ohio and Mississippi rivers fell to the English. A three-pronged attack against

French forces in the St. Lawrence/Great Lakes Region, launched in 1759, finally brought an end to the war. The fatal blow was struck at Quebec City. It resulted in an English victory remembered to this day by French Canadians as ***la conquête***, *the conquest*. The final battle was fought only a few months later when the English captured Montreal in the spring of 1760.

The **Treaty of Paris, 1763** made the conquest official. France surrendered all of its North American claims except for two small islands in the Gulf of St. Lawrence. The Louisiana territory west of the Mississippi was given to Spain for its help in the war against France. Everything else went to England, which now controlled a North American empire that stretched from the Atlantic Ocean to the Mississippi River and from Hudson Bay to the Gulf of Mexico. ■

A dying French General Montcalm is comforted and mourned by his troops while the battle for Quebec rages on in this painting by an adoring French artist.

Questions

1. Why was Acadia so important in the struggle for control of North America?

2. Why was population growth in New France so much slower than population growth in the English colonies?

3. Why did most of the Native Americans side with the French instead of the English in the struggle for control of North America?

4. Why did the British governor of Acadia force the colony's French inhabitants from their homeland during the 1750s?

5. WHAT DO YOU THINK? The story of New France is a story of missed opportunities by the French stretching over two centuries. What mistakes helped lead to the downfall of New France?

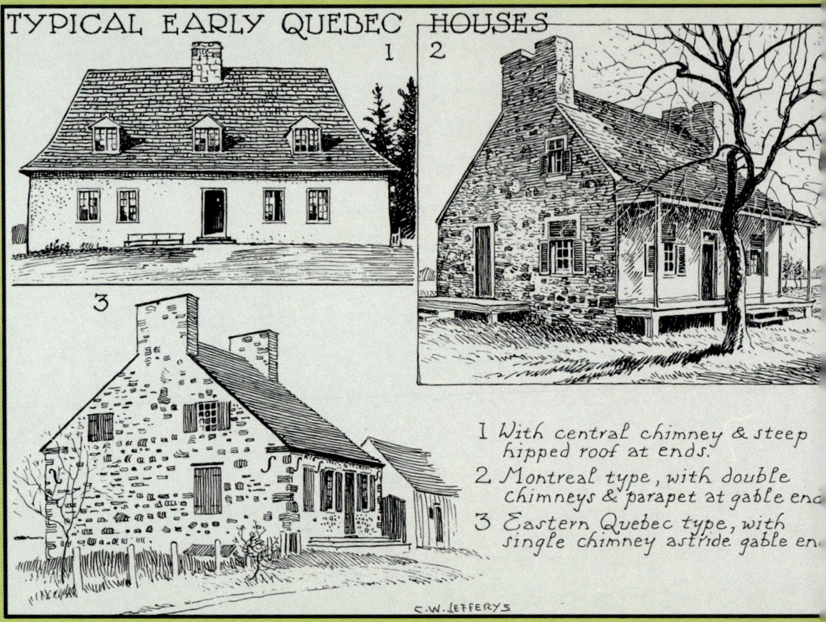

Typical early-Quebec houses.

17th century fireplace. Even the family dog helped with the cooking, turning the meat as it grilled over the open fire. The fireplace was the center of family life in both Canada and the United States for many centuries, especially during the winter months.

An early habitant farm near Quebec City.

SEIGNEURS AND HABITANTS

LIFE ALONG THE ST. LAWRENCE RIVER

ALL OF THE LAND in New France was owned by the King of France. Along the St.Lawrence River, large blocks of it were granted to privileged persons called *seigneurs*, who subdivided their *seigneuries* into small farm lots called *rotures*. These were settled by peasant farmers, or *habitants*. The farmers were required to share a portion of each year's harvest with the *seigneur* and were not allowed to own the land they farmed. But the *habitants* hardly seemed to mind, because they knew they were better off than the peasant farmers in France. Most had friendly and cooperative relationships with their *seigneurs*,and the extremely fertile soil of the St. Lawrence Valley provided plenty of food for everyone.

The St. Lawrence River was the lifeline of New France. Early farm lots were made long and narrow so that almost every family had frontage on the river. While remaining the most important waterway for the fur trade, the river was used by the *habitants* as a means of transportation when trading farm products with their neighbors and when visiting friends and attending church. The river was also their transportation route to Quebec City, which rapidly grew into the business and cultural center of New France.

Life in New France was dominated by the unifying force of the Catholic Church. Priests joined government officials or elected representatives in making the laws and setting taxes. The taxes were paid to both the Church and the government. While the French government managed the fur trade, the Catholic Church ruled over the *habitants* of New France.

Quebec City in 1683. The city was the religious, political, business and cultural capital of New France. The importance of the church in the life of early New France is reflected in the many crosses that are visible in the drawing.

CHAPTER 5

Early Years of English Rule

1763-1791

TO GUIDE YOUR READING
Look for answers to these questions

1. How did the end of the French and Indian War affect the 13 English colonies south of the Quebec Colony?
2. Why did England allow the people of Quebec to keep their French language and Catholic religion?
3. Why did the colonies in what is today Canada refuse to take part in the American Revolution?
4. How did the American Revolution affect Canada?

INTRODUCTION

The end of the French and Indian War brought mixed blessings to the English colonists in North America. For the first time in many years, people living in towns and cities could sleep at night without fear of being awakened by an attack on their homes. The bad news for many colonists, however, was that England could now turn its attention once again to the business of managing the affairs of its North American colonies. After having been neglected for so long a time, the sudden interference in their affairs by a distant government did not sit well with many people. New England merchants were especially angry because they were hit hardest by the new taxes and trade restrictions set by England to help pay for its war with France.

Only 12 years after the Treaty of Paris was signed, 13 of the 15 colonies in North America joined together and declared their independence from England, touching off the Revolutionary War. While war raged to the south, the colonists living in what would much later become Canada remained loyal to the king of England and welcomed thousands of people from the warring colonies who wanted to do the same.

SEEDS OF DISCONTENT

With French troops gone from the Ohio River Valley, most colonists felt sure that the way had been cleared for expansion west of the Appalachian Mountains. They were wrong. French presence or not, the Native peoples of the region had no intention of giving up their lands to the growing number of strange-looking settlers appearing from the east. In 1763, a group of tribes led by **Chief Pontiac** captured most of the English forts west of Niagara. England, having won control of the area after the French and Indian War, realized that it would have to take the Native peoples into account when setting policies in the New World. Therefore, King George III, in the **Royal Proclamation of 1763,** declared the land west of theAppalachians off limits for English settlement. The proclamation also created the **Quebec colony** from the former colony of New France. Hoping to

A frontier trader's store around 1780. The English takeover of Quebec soon brought change to the lives of French-Canadian families that remained in the St. Lawrence Valley, but daily frontier existence went on as usual.

encourage English settlement in Quebec, the king offered free land there to English veterans of the French and Indian War.

The Royal Proclamation may have pleased the Native peoples, but it angered the colonists who were now confined to a narrow strip of land along the Atlantic coast. The offer of free land in the Quebec colony was little consolation. Most English settlers were put off by its long winters and unfamiliar French culture. Only a handful took advantage of the offer. The colonists complained to the king, hoping he would change the proclamation, but he refused.

THE QUEBEC COLONY AFTER THE ENGLISH CONQUEST

Life in the Quebec colony changed very little after the English conquest. Instead of treating the French inhabitants as a defeated people, Governor General **James Murray** did everything he could to ease the change from French to English rule. His goodwill had a practical side. As unhappiness grew in many of England's other colonies, the English government knew it needed as many friends in North America as it could make.

The English government passed the **Quebec Act, 1774**. Its generous provisions allowed the French Canadians to maintain their language, culture and Roman Catholic religion. The church was allowed to keep the same powers it had exercized before the English takeover. The act also enlarged the boundaries of the Quebec colony south and west to include the vast and fertile territory between the Mississippi and Ohio rivers.

The Quebec Act was a major turning point in the history of North America. More than any other event, it determined that two separate nations would evolve from the English holdings there. It also ensured that French Canadian language and culture would remain alive in North America and would play an important role in shaping Canada's national identity.

The British bombardment of Quebec during the decisive battle of the Seven Years' War had devastating results. In addition to the human toll, many valuable paintings, tapestries and church properties were destroyed. These engravings were created by Canadian artist Charles William Jefferys based on a set of drawings made on the spot by a man named Richard Short.

The Quebec Act was welcomed by the French Canadians. But the people of the original 13 English colonies, most of whom belonged to Protestant churches, felt they had been betrayed by their king. Taxes imposed to help pay for the French and Indian War had already angered the colonists, but England's recognition of a French-speaking and Roman Catholic colony on their northern and western doorstep was the final straw. Colonial leaders met and quickly fired off an angry letter to the king. They complained about the new boundaries of Quebec and criticized the Roman Catholic Church in bitter terms, claiming that it had been allowed too much power in North America.

When once again their complaints were ignored by the king, more and more colonists in the lower 13 colonies talked of declaring independence from English rule. Fighting began in the spring of 1775, and independence was declared in 1776.

The Catholics

DISAGREEMENTS OVER RELIGION have often resulted in conflict between individuals and between countries. A lot of people take their belief in gods and religious teachings very seriously. There are many religious groups in the world today. and they all have different ideas about who and what a god is.

Members of the Christian religion follow the teachings of the man they call Jesus the Savior, or Christ, who lived during the days of the Roman Empire. Christians believe that Jesus was their god's son and that he was placed on Earth to teach people to live better lives by loving one other and by being less concerned with money and material things.

For 15 centuries, the number of people who were touched by the teachings of Jesus grew. As the influence of their religion spread, it became known as the Catholic, meaning universal, Church. Centered in Rome, Italy, its leader was called a Pope. Under the strong leadership of a line of Popes, the Roman Catholic Church expanded into most of Europe. Its leaders built beautiful cathedrals and gained millions of followers. By the time Columbus arrived in North America in 1492, almost all of Europe was Catholic.

But by then a split in the church was underway. Some Catholics had come to believe that their leaders, especially the Pope, had strayed from the original teachings of Jesus and had become too concerned with money and power. In the middle

and Protestants

of the 1500s, a Catholic priest in Germany named Martin Luther began a new Christian church that he claimed would more closely follow the teachings of Jesus. Soon, other Christians organized separate churches for similar reasons. Because they were protesting against the practices of the Catholic Church, they became known as *Protest*ants.

Soon, most countries in Europe were either all Catholic or all Protestant, depending on the choice of their King or Queen. As Europeans began settling in North America in the early 1600s, England, for example, was a Protestant country by order of King Henry VIII. Catholics who refused to become Protestant could be thrown in jail, or even put to death. France, Portugal and Spain, however, remained Catholic. In those countries, Protestants were treated as severely as Catholics were in England. Conflicts between the two groups became increasingly bitter. Each group was convinced that it was doing what God wanted and that God was on its side. There was little room for compromise. Bad feelings between Catholics and Protestants still remain in some parts of the world, such as Northern Ireland.

Catholics and Protestants who settled in North America brought their strong religious beliefs with them. Most of the English colonies were Protestant and the colonies of New France (and New Spain) were Catholic. Soon the conflict between Catholics and Protestants that had started in Europe began causing problems in North America as well.

french CANADIAN

FAVORITE WINTER RECIPES

Cream of Mushroom Soup

Wash and chop 1 & 1/4 pounds of fresh mushrooms. Chop 1 small onion and sauté in 5 tablespoons butter for 3 minutes. Add mushrooms and sauté for 5 minutes more. Stir in 5 tablespoons flour. Add 3 cups chicken broth and bring to a boil while stirring. Add salt and pepper to taste. Simmer for 30 minutes. Add 1 cup of whipping cream before serving. Makes 6 servings.

French-Canadian Pea Soup

1 pound dry yellow peas
2 & 1/2 quarts water
1/4 pound salt pork, cut into small pieces
3 onions, chopped
2 carrots, diced
small handful celery leaves
a few parsley twigs
3 bay leaves
1 teaspoon savory

Pour water over peas and let stand overnight. Add remaining ingredients and bring to a boil. Simmer for 2 or 3 hours, or until peas are soft.

Maple Syrup *Mousse*

1 cup maple syrup
4 eggs, separated
1 & 1/4 cups whipping cream

Beat egg yolks and syrup and heat over hot water until thickened. Cool. Whip cream and add to cooled syrup mixture. Beat egg whites and fold into this mixture. Freeze in 6-cup mold. Sprinkle toasted almonds over top.

Tourtiere (French-Canadian Meat Pie)

1 pound lean pork, minced
1 small onion, chopped
1 garlic clove
1 teaspoon salt
1/2 teaspoon savory
1/4 teaspoon cloves
1/3 cup chopped celery
3/4 cup finely chopped potatoes
pinch of cinnamon (to taste)
2 9-inch pie crusts

Fix all ingredients and bring to boil, then simmer for 30-40 minutes. Let cool. Pour into pie shell and cover with top crust. Bake at 400 degrees until golden brown. Serve hot with homemade fruit sauce, ketchup and pickles. Can be reheated or frozen and served later.

Maple Syrup Pie

1 cup maple syrup
1/3 cup water
3 tablespoons cornstarch
2 tablespoons butter
1/2 cup pecans
2 9-inch pie shells

Combine maple syrup and water and bring to boil. Mix cornstarch with a little water. Mix well into boiling syrup. Stir until smooth. Add butter and nuts. Pour into pie shell and cover with top crust. Make small cuts on top of crust. Bake for 20-30 minutes in 375-degree oven.

CANADA AND THE INDEPENDENCE MOVEMENT

Although they were invited to join the fight for independence, few people in the colonies that would become Canada had any reason to break their ties with England. With their Roman Catholic traditions and French language protected by the Quebec Act, people living in the Quebec colony had little to gain, and much to lose, by joining forces with the mostly Protestant and English-speaking colonies to the south. The letter written by colonial leaders protesting the Quebec Act left no doubt about how some of them felt about Roman Catholics.

Also, the farmers of Quebec were not affected by the trade restrictions and taxes that were causing such a fuss in New England. For generations, their way of life had remained almost unchanged and they had few complaints about the king or the governors he had sent to rule the colony.

The Nova Scotia colony was even less interested in joining the fight for independence. Because it was located closer to England than the other colonies, it enjoyed closer ties with that country. Also, Halifax was the site of a major English naval base.

CANADA IS INVADED

Canada, however, paid a heavy price for refusing to join the Revolution. In November of 1775, rebellious colonial soldiers led by **Richard Montgomery** invaded the Quebec colony and captured Montreal. After placing the city under military rule, Montgomery and his men headed down the St. Lawrence River to join forces with troops led by **Benedict Arnold** for an attack on Quebec City. The attack came during a blinding December snowstorm and was a dismal and costly failure. Montgomery lost his life along with more than 100 American soldiers. Arnold was wounded and 400 of his men were taken prisoner.

Attempts to regroup for another attack in the spring of 1776 ended when an English naval fleet carrying 10,000 reinforcements came sailing up the St. Lawrence. By the time the Americans left Quebec, whatever doubts the colonists there may have had about their future loyalties had disappeared. The revolutionaries had brought violence and bloodshed. They had even closed Roman Catholic churches in Montreal on Christmas Eve! Few people were sad to see them leave.

Despite the failures of their soldiers in the Quebec colony, the colonies that were about to become the United States won their independence after nearly eight years of war. In 1783, the new country won another important concession during a peace conference held in Paris. While loyal Quebec stood helplessly by, the fertile and fur-rich territory south of the Great Lakes, which had been part of the colony since 1774, was handed over to the United States.

The arrival of loyalists in the Nova Scotia colony. Many, like these folk in their fine clothing, were used to a comfortable city life in such places as Boston or New York. Their lives were radically changed in the wilds of their new homeland.

THE LOYALISTS CHANGE CANADA

About a third of the colonists living in what was to become the United States remained loyal to the King of England during the Revolution and refused to take up arms against him. They referred to themselves as **loyalists.** But to those who believed in and fought for independence, the loyalists were traitors. A number of their homes, among the finest in the colonies, were burned to the ground. Many loyalists were covered with tar and chicken feathers or were beaten. Some were even killed. After 1783, some 100,000 fled the United States. Many returned to England, but 60,000 settled in Nova Scotia and Quebec, including 10,000 African Americans.

Those headed for Nova Scotia gathered in New York City, Boston or almost any other Atlantic port where the British Navy could provide transportation. Many of these loyalists had been wealthy residents of New England or of the middle colonies and were used to comfortable surroundings.

They had a difficult time surviving in the wilderness of their new homeland. Some died trying.

Most loyalists who escaped to Nova Scotia settled together in the fertile area near the northern shore of the Bay of Fundy. In this place, where Acadia was first established, a community of 14,000 eventually managed to build a thriving colony far removed from Nova Scotia's original settlers and their government. In 1784, the region was marked off as a new colony, separate from the rest of the Nova Scotia peninsula, and named **New Brunswick**.

Not all of the loyalists left the United States by sea. A large number traveled on foot from the frontier regions of New England, New York and Pennsylvania to the southernmost areas of western Quebec. They settled in the upper St. Lawrence Valley close to the Great Lakes. Unlike the townspeople who had fled to Nova Scotia after the war, most of these western Loyalists were rugged farm

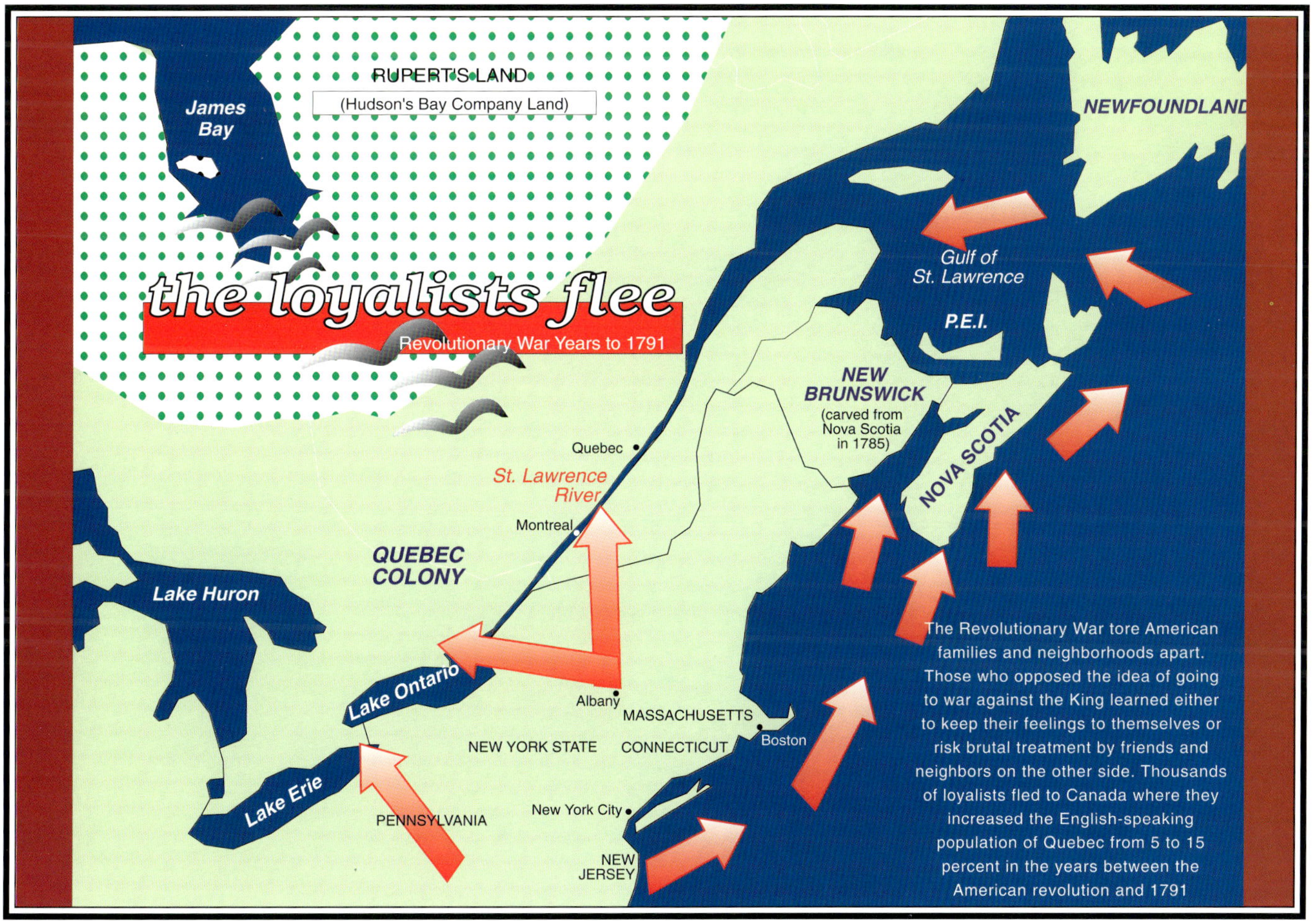

folk, better prepared for the hard work required to carve out a home and a livelihood from the wilderness. Still, it wasn't easy. As one wrote:

....the whole country was forest which had to be subdued by the axe and toil. For a while we led a primitive life and, with a few poles and brushwood, formed our tents on the Indian plan.

The most trying period of our lives was the year 1788, called the year of scarcity. . . . All the crops failed. . . . For several days we were without food except that the various roots we found and boiled down to nourish us. We noticed what roots the pigs eat and by that means avoided anything that had poisonous qualities. . . . our poor dog was killed to allay the pangs of hunger; the very idea made some people sick, but others devoured the flesh quite ravenous.

UPPER CANADA AND LOWER CANADA

The western loyalists formed a new English-speaking and Protestant community in western

one LOYALIST family's tale

THE SAD TALE OF FILOR DRIBLEE of Long Island was revealed in a letter written by his wife Polly to her brother in England. It is a chilling example of how disruptive and divisive the American Revolution was to ordinary Americans—especially those who decided to remain loyal to the Crown.

According to the letter, the Driblee family home was robbed and vandalized by rebels. Polly and her five children were stripped of their clothing and sent "naked into the streets." The family was "plundered (robbed) and stripped" twice more before making it to New Brunswick. After having spent six months in jail during the war, Mr. Driblee took his life within a year of arriving in St. John. Soon after that, Polly and her children lost two-log cabin homes to fire in a year's time. She also wrote:

I assure you, my dear Billy, that many have been the day since my arrival in this inhospitable country, that I should have thought myself and family truly happy could we have had (just one decent meal). . . . I could have borne these burdens of Loyalty with fortitude had not my poor children cried, "Mama, why don't you help me and give me bread?"

Quebec, far from where the colony's original French settlers lived. Soon the government of England, as it had done earlier in Nova Scotia, created a separate colony for the loyalists. The **Constitution Act, 1791** divided Quebec into two colonies and named them **Upper Canada** and **Lower Canada**. Lower Canada was located in the St. Lawrence Lowlands east and north of the Ottawa River, the area where most French Canadians lived. Upper Canada was the territory west and north of lakes Erie and Ontario that had been settled by the loyalists.

The settlement of both Nova Scotia and Upper Canada changed the course of Canadian history. The differences between Canada and the United States, which were already set apart by language and culture, became even greater after the loyalists arrived. Having placed themselves on opposite sides of the war for independence, Canadians and Americans now found themselves on opposite sides of a new set of borders. Those borders separated two very different peoples now traveling very different roads to nationhood.

One of the earliest maps of Upper Canada.

Questions

1. Why did the Proclamation of 1763 anger the colonists in England's original 13 colonies?
2. Why did the people of the Quebec Colony have little interest in joining the American Revolution?
3. Who were the loyalists and how did they affect Canada?
4. How did the loyalists who settled in the area of the upper St.Lawrence River Valley and the Great Lakes *differ* from the original inhabitants of the Quebec colony?
5. WHAT DO YOU THINK? With thousands of Protestant and English-speaking loyalists pouring into the Quebec colony after the war, what problems may develop as a result of the provisions of the Quebec Act?

CHAPTER 6

The Road to Nationhood

1791-1867

The first Canadian postage stamp, issued in February, 1851.

TO GUIDE YOUR READING
Look for answers to these questions

1. Why did the United States invade Canada in 1812?
2. How did the War of 1812 change Canada?
3. How did Canada move towards self-government during the 1800s?

INTRODUCTION

In the years following the Revolutionary War, the colonies in Canada remained under British rule. But many Americans believed that it was only a matter of time before Canada would become part of the United States. That belief was one reason why the United States fought the ***War of 1812*** *with Great Britain.*

Canadians, however, had no intention of joining the United States. By 1800, the differences between Canadians and Americans were clear. For one thing, more than half of Canadians were French and Roman Catholic. Also, most English Canadians were loyalists whose families had left the United States rather than fight against their king. These Canadians still had bitter feelings towards the United States because of the way loyalists had been treated during and after the American Revolution.

The successful defense of Canada from the American invasion of 1812 united French and English

Canadians with a sense of common purpose and pride. However different each group was from the other, both were even more different from the people of the United States. This much they had in common. For most of its history, the desire to remain separate from the United States has been like a glue holding Canada together.

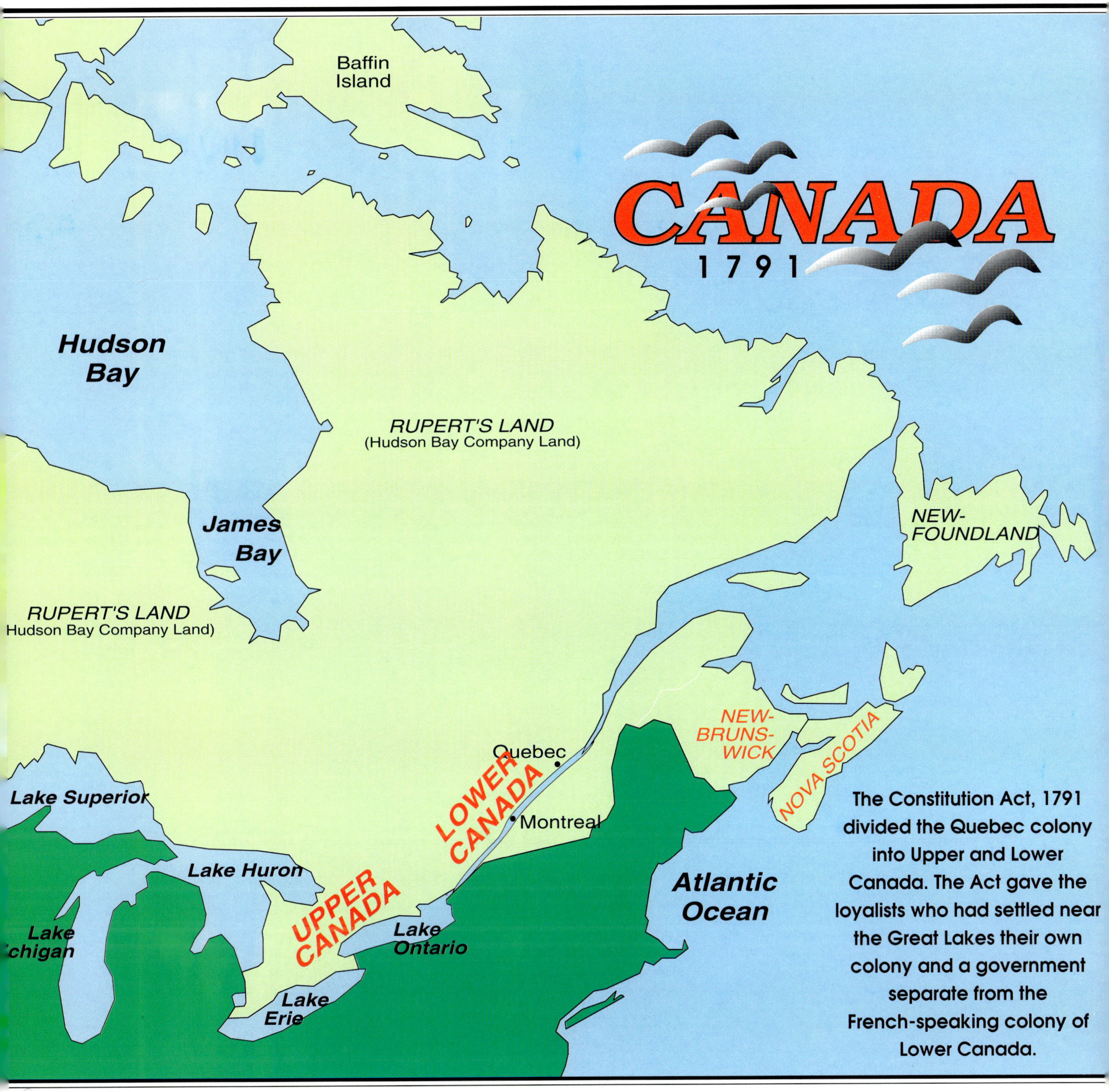

The Constitution Act, 1791 divided the Quebec colony into Upper and Lower Canada. The Act gave the loyalists who had settled near the Great Lakes their own colony and a government separate from the French-speaking colony of Lower Canada.

THE WAR OF 1812

The defeat of France by Great Britain in 1763 did not end the long rivalry between the two world powers. By 1800, they were fighting again. The United States tried to avoid becoming involved in the conflict, but that proved impossible. The French attacked American ships bound for England and the British attacked American ships bound for France. Many American sailors were snatched from their boats and forced to serve in the British Navy. The practice, called impressment, outraged the citizens of the United States.

Many Americans believed that their country should take advantage of Great Britain's problems with France and attack Canada. Members of Congress who favored such an action were known as **war hawks.** They wanted revenge against the British and hoped to gain valuable new territory for the United States. A victory would also prevent the British from invading the United States from Canada.

Leader of the British forces, General Brock, meets his Native American ally, Shawnee Chief Tecumseh.

Chief Tecumseh leads his warriors against the Americans at the Battle of the Thames, in southern Ontario, 1814.

War hawk Senator Henry Clay told the United States Senate that,

the conquest of Canada is in your power. I trust I shall not be thought bold when I state that I truly believe that the militia of Kentucky are alone competent to place Montreal and Upper Canada at your feet.

Clay was wrong. The 1812 invasion of Canada failed. He and the other war hawks had badly underestimated how strongly Canadians felt about remaining separate from the United States. Though greatly outnumbered, the Canadians put up a fierce fight in defense of their homeland. They received valuable help from Shawnee **Chief Tecumseh** and his army of Native Americans who joined the battle hoping to block further westward expansion by the United States. Canada's success in turning back the invasion was a source of great pride and gave Canadians their first indication of what it might be like to be part of a nation.

In this naval battle fought during the War of 1812, the warship United States captures the Macedonia.

October 13, 1813: Canada won a major victory at Queenston Heights, near Niagara Falls, but lost the brilliant General Brock.

However united in their desire to remain separate from the United States, Canadians remained divided by language and culture. As the populations of both Upper and Lower Canada grew, so did problems between French and English Canadians. Hoping to achieve greater harmony between the two groups, the British government decided to erase the boundary between English and French Canada. The **Act of Union, 1841** joined Upper Canada and Lower Canada to create a single new colony named the **United Canadas**. Unfortunately, the differences between French and English Canadians were too great just to disappear like a line on a map.

SLAVERY AND THE AMERICAN CIVIL WAR AFFECT CANADA

Almost from the beginning of European settlement in North America, and particularly in the southern United States, much of the hard work of clearing and farming the land was done by enslaved people kidnapped from their African

This cartoon, published in London around 1820, pokes fun at those settlers who were taken in by dishonest land sharks promising great deals in Canadian real estate.

homelands and then bought and sold like farm animals. Slavery flourished in the United States well into the 1860s, but the practice was outlawed in the British Empire in 1834.

Under the cover of darkness and with their eyes fixed on the North Star, some 40,000 slaves escaped from their owners and headed for freedom in Canada. The help they received along the way from the people who participated in the so-called **Underground Railroad** angered slave owners and helped bring the argument over slavery to a boil.

In 1860, **Abraham Lincoln** was elected President of the United States. Right after taking his oath of office, Lincoln repeated his campaign pledge to oppose the spread of slavery into any more territory of the United States. Within weeks, 11 southern states, where slavery had been a way of life for more than 200 years, declared their independence. They formed a separate country and named it the **Confederate States of America.** President Lincoln's attempt to force the rebellious

Home life in rural Quebec during the 1800s is illustrated in this 1852 painting by popular Canadian artist Cornelius Krieghoff. The wood stove was the family's only appliance. The rug was woven from rags.

states to remain part of the United States resulted in a bitter and bloody conflict known as the **American Civil War**.

During this civil war, the British colonies in Canada were more than interested bystanders. The war put a severe strain on relations between Great Britain and what remained of the United States. In their hearts, most people in Great Britain favored the north because of its opposition to slavery. But President Lincoln's attempt to prevent the South from selling cotton to Great Britain almost brought the British into the war on the side of the Confederate States. Had that happened, Canada might have become one of the war's battlefields—and one of its casualties. Canadians held their breath as some Americans talked of allowing the rebellious southern states to go their separate way and of taking Canada to make up for the loss.

The British did not formally join the war and Canada was not invaded. The army of the North managed to defeat the Confederate army in 1865 and the United States was reunited.

Like so many before and after them, this couple poses for a souvenir photo in front of Niagara Falls, 1859. The falls frame the Canada-United States border near Lake Ontario and are a favorite spot for honeymooners and families on vacation.

But Canada's sigh of relief was short-lived. Its colonies were weaker and more divided than ever before. Attempts to build railways to link them had left their governments deeply in debt. In such a condition, they presented an inviting target for an invasion by the United States.

THE BRITISH NORTH AMERICA ACT ESTABLISHES THE DOMINION OF CANADA

In 1864, the French and English leaders of the United Canadas joined the leaders of Nova Scotia and New Brunswick at **Charlottetown, Prince Edward Island** to discuss the possibility of greater unity between their colonies. They also hoped to gain more independence from Great Britain. Within three years, they completed a plan to bring them together under one government with each colony still able to control most of its own affairs. The arrangement was known as a **confederation**.

The Fathers of Confederation help to hammer out the final details of the British North America Act in London, England, 1866.

Many, especially English Canadians, opposed the plan because they had few complaints about British rule. Still, as one Canadian leader put it:

the question is as simple as this—we must either have confederation or be taken over by the United States.

Canada's desire for greater independence was welcomed and even encouraged by the British. By this time, Great Britain had colonies on five continents and most of them were far more profitable than its colonies in North America. So, in 1867, the British government approved the confederation plan and made it law by passing the **British North America Act**. The huge United Canadas colony was divided to create the provinces of **Ontario** and **Quebec** which then joined **Nova Scotia** and **New Brunswick** to create a new nation named the **Dominion of Canada**. Prince Edward Island joined six years later.

By providing a framework for the government of Canada, the British North America Act served as Canada's first constitution. The new country, however, was not completely independent. Under the act, Great Britain still had the final word in Canadian affairs. ■

Questions

1. What two goals did the War Hawks hope to achieve by invading Canada in 1812?
2. How did America's Civil War threaten Canada?
3. What was the result of the British North America Act?
4. WHAT DO YOU THINK? In what ways was the War of 1812 a major turning point in Canadian history?

Women

These women are taking a rare break from their chores to visit together at a house in Grand Prairie, Alberta.

IT IS ALMOST IMPOSSIBLE to imagine how women once lived and were treated in both the United States and Canada. Discouraged by men from participating in many of the kinds of activities that are recorded in most history books, women still played an essential—and exhausting—role in the settlement and development of both countries.

Many of the earliest women colonists to settle in New France were young girls known as *les filles du roi*, or "the King's daughters." They had been recruited after 1665 as potential wives for the colony's overwhelmingly male population. These women, and those who had settled earlier, built small businesses and established hospitals and schools. Many, too, braved the wild interior of North America as dedicated missionaries. Colonial and frontier women often worked with their husbands, trapping, hunting and clearing land. Much of the time they were doing this hard physical work, they were pregnant or caring for young children—or both.

There is evidence that by the 1820s some women had found their way into a number of nontraditional careers such as mining and woodworking. But the goal of most women during the 1800s was motherhood. Training began at an early age.

Young girls in that century spent most of their time at their mothers' side preparing for the roles of housewife and mother. Very few were allowed to play cards or to participate in the rough-and-tumble games that boys were permitted to play. They were dressed by their mothers in frilly skirts

# of Early Canada

and bows and encouraged to play with dolls well into their teens. The books they were given to read, such as *The Holiday Album for Girls*, featured ideal heroines who passed on messages about proper manners and behavior. Another favorite book in the late 1800s was *The Young Lady's Book; A Manual of Amusements, Exercises, Studies and Pursuits*. Among other things, the book discouraged girls from trying their hand at chess because it "is not a game much played by ladies as it requires rather more thought and calculation than women possess." That advice was written by a woman.

Before the 1900s, the majority of Americans and Canadians lived on farms. Many spent their entire lives in the same house, first as youngsters, then as parents and then as grandparents—if they were fortunate enough to avoid the many sicknesses, accidents and infections that claimed the lives of many children before their 10th birthday. For women, being a homemaker and mother was more than a full-time job. Cooking filled almost every hour that was not spent taking care of children. Between cleaning, chopping, cutting, mixing and stirring the various farm products that would become the family's next meal, women had to prepare all of their own staples such as bread, butter, pickles, mustard, ketchup and preserves.

A frontier woman, shovel in hand, poses in front of the family's new homestead. One of the men in the photo is likely her husband, the others may be sons, or hired hands, or both.

Women also made most of the family's clothing, as well as a variety of home products such as rat poison, ink, silver cleaner, cold cream, tooth powder, hair tonic, candles and soap. In most families, mother also doubled as the family doctor, treating ailments using a variety of home remedies learned from her own mother years before.

CHAPTER 7

The Nation Grows

This portrait of Canada's first Prime Minister, John A. Macdonald, was taken near the end of his long career.

1867-present

TO GUIDE YOUR READING
Look for answers to these questions

1. What difficulties did Canadians encounter as they tried to move westward?
2. How was the westward expansion of Canada affected by events in the United States?
3. Why was the transcontinental railroad so important to the development of Canada?
4. Why have Canada and the United States become such close friends in this century?

INTRODUCTION

While their American neighbors moved westward, building roads and canals through the fertile Ohio and Mississippi river valleys, Canadians found themselves hemmed in by the enormous expanse of Great Lakes waters and the Canadian Shield. Many dreamed of a day when a transcontinental railroad would open the prairie to settlement and unite the nation by linking the provinces of eastern Canada with Britain's most distant North American colony, British Columbia.

There was little time to waste. As the westward expansion of the United States reached the Rocky Mountains, many Americans looked north for their next frontier. Some suggested that the area should be settled and made a state. Texas, once a province of Mexico, had become part of the United States this way in the 1840s.

Canada's first Prime Minister, ***John A. Macdonald****, had other ideas. He immediately began working toward the goal of bringing the remaining British holdings west and north of Ontario under the control of the Canadian government.*

By the turn of the twentieth century, thanks largely to the policies of Prime Minister Macdonald, Canada extended from ocean to ocean. Having finally established itself as a permanent fixture in North America, Canada now turned its attention to the task of building a friendly relationship with its giant neighbor to the south.

PRIME MINISTER MACDONALD TAKES CHARGE AND BUILDS A RAILROAD

In July, 1868, at Prime Minister Macdonald's urging, Great Britain transferred the huge territory controlled by the Hudson's Bay Company to Canada. The land, known as Rupert's Land, included what would later become the prairie provinces and the northern territories. The colony of British Columbia on the west coast was next. Like the eastern colonies before Confederation, British Columbia was deeply in debt and was receiving little support from Great Britain. Macdonald's government promised to take over the colony's debts and to build a railway linking it with the rest of the country. In return, British Columbia agreed, in 1871, to become a province.

In 1878, Prime Minister Macdonald announced a three-point program for Canada called the **National Policy**. It included a plan to promote the growth of industry in the East, another plan to encourage **immigration** to the West and money to construct the transcontinental railroad that had been promised British Columbia.

Laying railroad track over the 1500 miles of rocks, swamps and lakes of the Canadian Shield

A young girl and her mother, members of the Assiniboine tribe of the southern prairies, are photographed next to their beautifully hand-painted tipi.

Constructing railroads during the 1800s was backbreaking work. Explosives were used to blast through solid rock, but the rest of the job had to be finished by workers using steam-powered jackhammers and simple picks and shovels.

between Toronto and Winnipeg was no easy task. And even with that accomplished, the railroad builders were only halfway to British Columbia with the Canadian Rockies still to cross. The successful completion of the **Canadian Pacific Railway** in 1885, years ahead of schedule, was one of the great engineering feats of the 19th century. It was also a tribute to Prime Minister Macdonald's leadership and vision. When a lack of private funds threatened to derail the project, he convinced the Canadian government to spend public money to keep it on track.

A five-million-dollar government loan saved the railroad, and the decision to grant it set an important example that future governments of Canada would follow. Because of the country's huge size and small population, the Canadian government has taken an active role in developing resources and building transportation and communication systems. This has been achieved by creating government-owned businesses known as **crown corporations**. Canada's oldest and largest radio and television network, for example, the Canadian Broadcasting Corporation (CBC), is owned by the government. So is a major petroleum company called PetroCanada and also the Canadian National Railway (CNR).

The Last SPIKE

The last spike in Canada's transcontinental railroad is pounded in place at Eagle Pass, British Columbia. This photograph is one of the most famous in Canadian history, but no one is sure who took it. The exciting event took place at 9:30 in the morning of November 7, 1885.

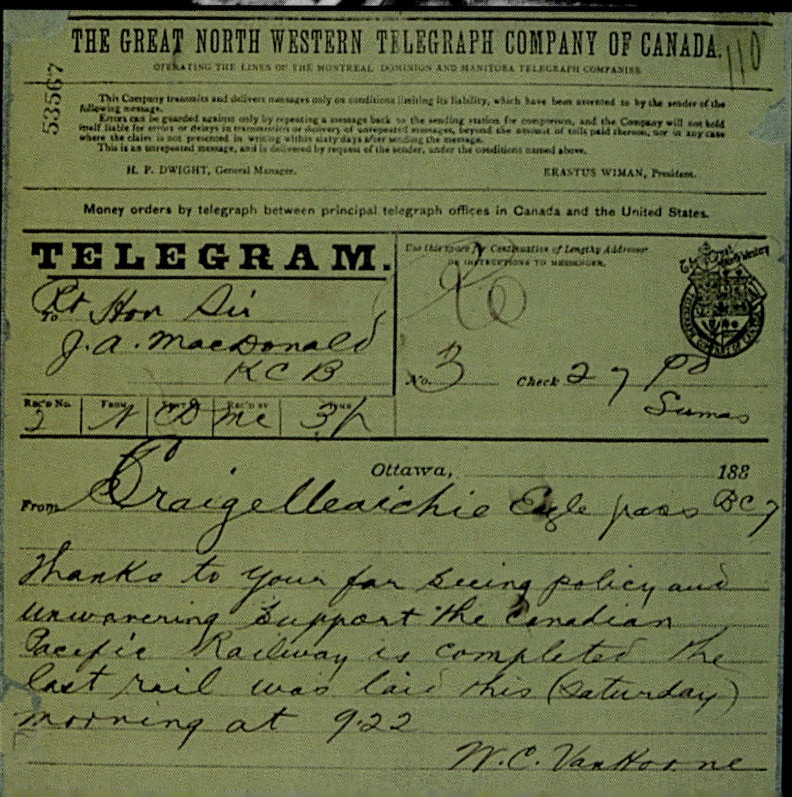

THE GREAT NORTH WESTERN TELEGRAPH COMPANY OF CANADA.

OPERATING THE LINES OF THE MONTREAL DOMINION AND MANITOBA TELEGRAPH COMPANIES.

53567

This Company transmits and delivers messages only on conditions limiting its liability, which have been assented to by the sender of the following message.

Errors can be guarded against only by repeating a message back to the sending station for comparison, and the Company will not hold itself liable for errors or delays in transmission or delivery of unrepeated messages, beyond the amount of tolls paid thereon, nor in any case where the claim is not presented in writing within sixty days after sending the message.

This is an unrepeated message, and is delivered by request of the sender, under the conditions named above.

H. P. DWIGHT, General Manager. ERASTUS WIMAN, President.

Money orders by telegraph between principal telegraph offices in Canada and the United States.

TELEGRAM.

To Rt Hon Sir J. A. MacDonald KCB

No. 3 Check 27 pd Sumas

Ottawa, 188

From Craigellachie Eagle pass BC

Thanks to your far seeing policy and unwavering support the Canadian Pacific Railway is completed the last rail was laid this (Saturday) morning at 9:22

W. C. VanHorne

This telegram was sent to Prime Minister Macdonald to inform him that the "last spike" had been driven. Coast-to-coast service began in June, 1886.

A locomotive being assembled by hand in 1858, before the days of mass production.

SETTLING CANADA'S WEST

The Canadian Shield was not the only obstacle to westward expansion. The Native peoples who lived on the eastern edge of the prairies, the **Métis,** gave early government surveyors a chilly reception. Descended from the early French fur traders who had married Native wives, the Métis had developed a unique culture that combined both sides of their heritage. Several hundred Métis were living in what is today southeastern Manitoba when agents of the Canadian government arrived to pave the way for new settlement. Fearing for the future of their French language and Roman Catholic religion—not to mention their land—the Métis decided to resist any attempt to bring new people to the West.

A Métis encampment at Dog's Head Lake near Winnipeg, Manitoba. These cone-shaped dwellings, known as tipis, were constructed out of poles and animal hides.

Under their leader, **Louis Riel**, they seized a Hudson's Bay Company fort and tried to scare away any settlers who ventured into the region. One newcomer lost his life in a skirmish near Fort Gary, where Winnipeg is today. The resistance ended with the help of Roman Catholic Bishop Taché, who convinced the government of Canada to compromise with the Métis. The result was the **Manitoba Act, 1870**, in which the government would add a new province to the map of Canada but with the promise to protect French language and culture there. Many Métis, including Louis Riel, wanted no part of the agreement. They packed their belongings and headed farther west, searching for a new home where they would be left alone.

Louis Riel

But it was only 15 years before westward expansion caught up with the Métis again, this time in what is today southern **Alberta** and **Saskatchewan**. As they had done before, the Métis looked to Louis Riel to lead their fight against the government of Canada. Once again, Riel encouraged raids against military outposts, trading centers and homes built by the new settlers. He and his followers even ambushed a group of **Northwest Mounted Police**, who had been stationed in western Canada to maintain law and order while the region developed.

Prime Minister Macdonald ordered Canadian soldiers to put down this uprising, called the **Northwest Rebellion**. Riel was arrested and tried for treason. Despite pleas from the Roman Catholic church and French Canadians throughout the country, Riel was found guilty and put to death by hanging.

The capture of Louis Riel by scouts of the Northwest Mounted Police, May 15, 1885. Riel was found guilty of treason and was put to death by hanging.

The story of Louis Riel is one of the most controversial in Canadian history. Although he was found guilty of treason, his bravery on behalf of the Métis made him a hero to French-speaking Canadians who were feeling more and more threatened by the rapid expansion of English Canada.

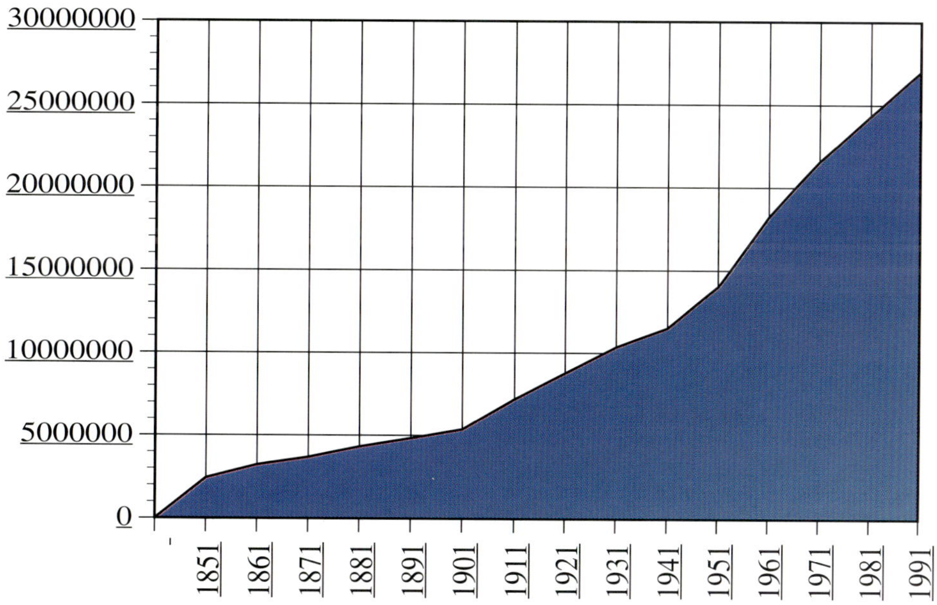

Population Growth — 1851-1991

A class picture taken in 1887 in Muskoka Lakes, Ontario. Students of different ages and grade levels were taught in the same one-room schoolhouse by a single teacher.

HARDSHIPS IN WESTERN CANADA

Although Prime Minister Macdonald's government managed to take control of the West, attempts to encourage immigrants from other nations to settle there met with little success. Despite expensive advertising campaigns in Great Britain and the United States, only a few immigrants came to Canada during Macdonald's years as Prime Minister and even fewer headed across the country to establish farms in western Canada. The long, bitter winters and short growing season made life there unappealing and even dangerous. One settler who tried to farm in western Ontario and then gave up, wrote:

I bought a lot of wild land, but found I had been deceived. I lived for two months in a shed they called a shanty, eaten alive by mosquitoes. I could get nothing to eat but salt pork. All my English farming knowledge was quite useless. It broke my heart to work among stumps and never see a well-plowed field. . . .

Farther west, the sod covering the prairie was so thick that it was almost impossible to till

This advertising truck cruised the streets of London, England during the early 1900s urging people to settle in western Canada.

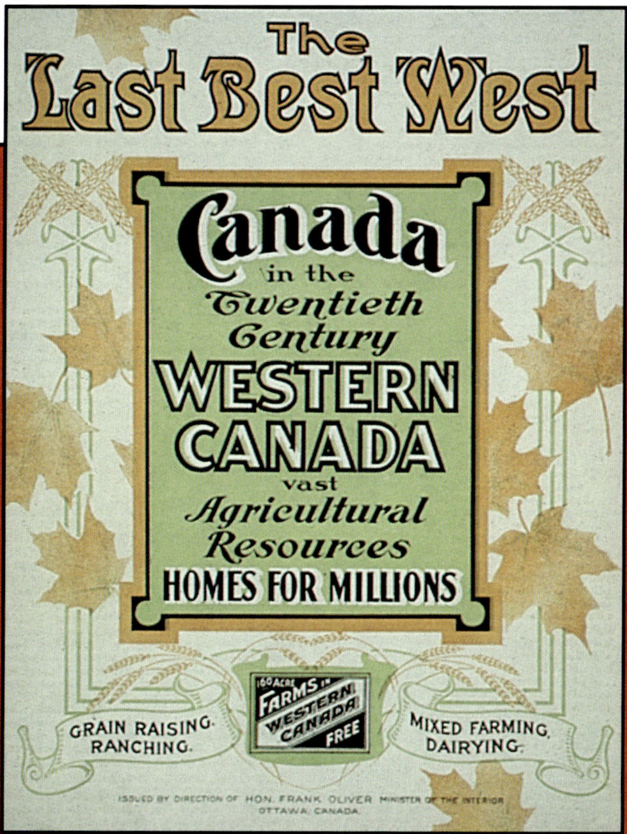

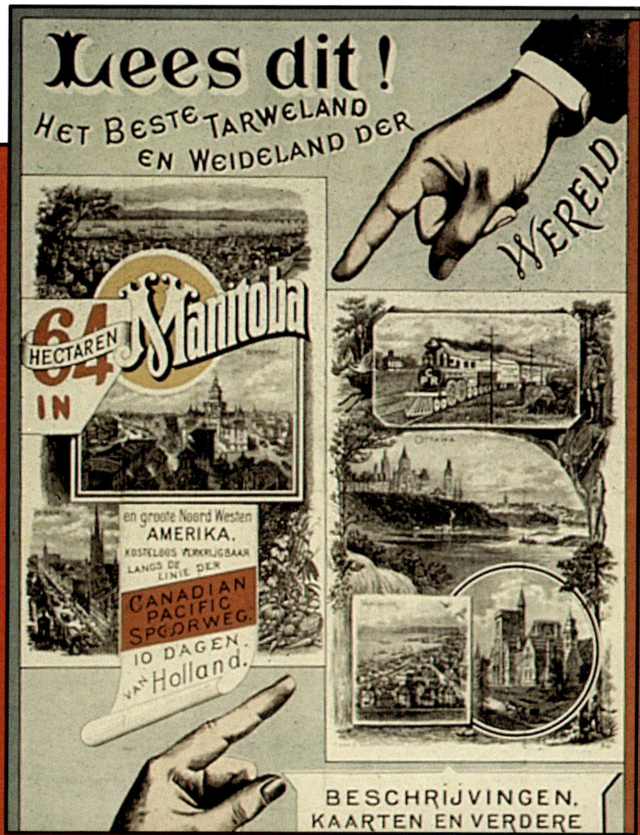

Posters like these were used to lure settlers to western Canada from many European countries during the late 1800s and early 1900s.

with the traditional wooden plows brought by the first farmers.

At the beginning of the 20th century, the country's first French-Canadian Prime Minister, **Sir Wilfrid Laurier**, stepped up the effort to make life in the West more desirable and to lure new settlers to Canada. His government sent agents carrying thousands of posters and pamphlets to Europe and the United States to advertise free land in, and travel assistance to, "the last, best West." The government built grain elevators on the prairies and supplied money for a second railroad system to encourage settlement beyond the border-hugging Canadian Pacific line. New, more hardy strains of wheat, along with steel plows and other advances in farm machinery, helped to make farming less risky and more profitable. Finally, the immigrants came.

A father and his sons ready their farm with three horses, an ax and a plow.

Many of the buildings that went up during the gold-rush days are still standing. Curious tourists let their imaginations run wild: "What was it like when this lunch house was packed with noisy prospectors paying for caribou burgers with glittering gold dust?"

Prospectors who came to the Yukon by way of Alaska had to cross Chikoot Pass to get to the gold fields. Agents of the Northwest Mounted Police required miners to have at least a year's rations before they could pass. It took many trips over the top before the miners could get all their supplies to the other side.

YOU WOULD HARDLY KNOW IT by visiting the place today, but a century ago the sleepy, lightly populated and out-of-the-way Klondike region of the Yukon Territory was one of the busiest and wildest places in Canada. The 1896 discovery of gold nuggets in the Yukon River set off a gold rush that attracted some 60,000 prospectors from all over the world, all of whom hoped to strike it rich. In just two years, Dawson City, located in the region, grew from a settlement of only a few houses to a city of more than 20,000 people, most of them men—*rugged* men. By 1921, the gold was gone and so were the prospectors. Dawson's population dwindled to fewer than a thousand people.

GOLD *fever*

Between 1897 and 1904, more than a hundred million dollars worth of gold was hauled out of the Klondike. The take in 1900 alone was 22 million dollars.

The easy-to-get-at gold in the creek beds was gathered by scooping up panfulls of gravel and shaking the pan to separate the gravel from the gold nuggets. It took a trained eye because most of the nuggets were unpolished and hard to distinguish from other pebbles and stones in the gravel. The gold that was just lying around in the creek beds was soon panned out. Larger amounts of gold could be mined, but mining in the Klondike was difficult. Just inches below the surface, the ground was frozen solid all year long. Steam thawing was the most popular method of dealing with the permafrost. Iron pipes were driven into the ground and steam was forced through holes in the pipes, thawing the soil and gravel so it could be sifted and searched for gold.

Panning for gold in the Yukon.

buffalo *tails*

Buffalo captured by the Métis provided food, clothing and other essentials.

As the railroad was constructed across the prairie, more and more buffalo were killed for their meat and for sport. Their bones were gathered and shipped to eastern Canada where they were turned into fertilizer. The fact that the buffalo was nearly extinct by the late 1800s destroyed the way of life of many tribes of Native peoples on the prairie.

Home Children

These British children, who were either orphaned or had families too poor to support them, were called home children. Thousands were sent to Canada for adoption between the 1860s and 1930s. Some of the adoptions worked out well, but too many people took advantage of the program to get free labor. Some of the children died from overwork or starvation.

THE IMMIGRANT EXPERIENCE

While thousands of Europeans took advantage of the generous land offers in the Canadian West, most immigrants to Canada settled in the nation's eastern cities. Others found low-paying jobs on farms or in the forests and mines. The experience of newcomers to Canada was similar to that of people moving to the United States. Many became victims of prejudice and discrimination. Immigrants from eastern Europe, Asia, Africa and the Caribbean often felt as unwelcome in Canada as they did in the United States. For many years Canadians, like Americans, preferred their immigrants to be white, English-speaking and Protestant. The man in charge of Prime Minister Laurier's immigration policies scolded Canadians who held such views. In 1901, he wrote,

the cry against non-British immigrants is the most ignorant and absurd thing I have ever heard. I despise racial prejudice because it is not based on reason. You can excite the hatred of a nationality against another simply by hammering away and appealing to their prejudices. In the course of time you will work up an excitement. I cannot imagine a more ignorant and unpatriotic policy.

A German family arrives in Quebec City in 1911.

When Canada became a country in 1867, it joined Newfoundland, (which did not become part of Canadian Confederation until 1949), Australia, New Zealand and South Africa as dominions in the British Commonwealth. As such, the countries had control over their internal affairs but remained tied to Great Britain in a mutual defense agreement.

Foot soldiers in Europe during World War I spent much of their time in trenches like this one. The trenches were damp and dirty. Most of the men wound up with foot infections from standing in the muck. Lice, ticks and scalp infections were also common.

A NEW RELATIONSHIP WITH THE UNITED STATES

As Canada and the United States moved into the 20th century, relations between the two countries were cool. The American invasion in 1812 had left deep scars. During the rest of the 1800s, speeches by American politicians calling for the annexation of Canada were a constant reminder that the United States remained a threat to Canada's survival. As late as 1890, one American official referred to Canada as "an apple waiting to fall into the American basket."

A dispute in 1903 over the boundary between Canada and **Alaska** caused more problems. President Theodore Roosevelt made matters worse when he ordered American troops to the Alaskan border while representatives of the two countries were meeting to settle the dispute without the use of force.

But **World War I**, which began in 1914, became an important turning point in the Canada-United States relationship. With Great Britain under attack by Germany and its allies, Canada, as a member of the **British Commonwealth of Nations**, immediately joined the war effort. The

United States tried to remain neutral, but it could not. With its ships under attack by German submarines and democracy threatened in Great Britain and France, the United States finally decided to enter the conflict in 1917. It sent millions of young soldiers, sailors and pilots across the Atlantic to fight. The additional forces were too much for the enemy to handle and the war ended a year later. Canadian and American troops returned home as friends and allies, ready to help build a new relationship between their two countries.

During World War I, posters were used both to recruit soldiers and to ask the Canadian people to support the forces fighting the war by making sacrifices at home.

Canada paid a very high price for its participaton in World War I. However glorious the war may have appeared on the posters at home, nearly 61,000 Canadians lost their lives. Canada suffered a greater proportion of losses than any other country. Many bodies were shipped home to be buried in graves like these at the Seventh Battalion Cemetery in British Columbia.

School children during the 1930s looked forward to after-school hours when they could listen to the family radio.

Canada and the United States were soon cooperating in many ways. American companies opened manufacturing plants in Canada, providing jobs and products for Canadians to buy. American money helped Canada develop its natural resources, many of which were purchased by manufacturers in the United States. Soon the two countries were each other's most important trade partners. They still are.

Traveling in the 1930s

A train guard, in 1933, sells goggles in an open observation car to protect passengers from coal dust pouring from the train's engine.

Buses like this one on the Gaspé Peninsula in the Gulf of St. Lawrence offered coast-to-coast service with many stops along the way in both Canada and the United States.

Posters appeared throughout Canada to boost morale during World War II, as they had during World War I. Many of them urged the Canadian people to support the forces fighting the war by making sacrifices at home.

World War II brought them even closer together. Now the sons and daughters of the Canadians and Americans who had fought in WWI were called upon to defend democracy in Europe, under attack for the second time in fewer than 25 years. Again, the enemy was Germany, led by the Nazi dictator Adolph Hitler, along with a powerful Italy, led by another dictator, Benito Mussolini. Canada answered the call immediately following Great Britain's declaration of war against Germany in September, 1939. At first, the United States tried to remain neutral. Any hope that it could do so evaporated on the morning of December 7, 1941 when planes of the Japanese air force attacked the American navel base at Pearl Harbor, Hawaii. Within days, the United States was at war in both Europe and Asia. The war raged for almost four more years, spreading into Russia, eastern Europe and northern Africa. The most decisive battle of the war in Europe was fought on the beaches of Normandy,

Johnny Canuck became a popular comic book hero during WWII. Canadians were filled with pride as the handsome and brave Johnny outwitted sinister war villian, Adolph Hitler, in a series of daring adventures.

France, on June 6, 1944, D-Day. The battle to free France was waged by troops of Canada, Great Britain and the United States. Thousands lost their lives in the daring and heroic effort.

In the years following World War II, Canada found itself sandwiched between two quarreling nuclear powers, the United States and what was then the Soviet Union. Knowing that any war between those two countries would take place right over their heads, Canadians worked with the United States and the United Nations to prevent a nuclear war. Canada joined the United States to form the **North American Aerospace Command (NORAD)**. The arrangement integrated the air defense forces of both countries under a single command.

The **St. Lawrence Seaway** project was another cooperative venture between the United States and Canada. The seaway, opened in 1959, allows large, ocean-going vessels to use the St. Lawrence River as a link between the Atlantic Ocean and the Great Lakes. Until it was built, only small ships could travel the river between Montreal and Lake Ontario because that stretch of water was shallow and filled with dangerous rapids.

A boat headed for the Great Lakes approaches Bridge 13 on the Welland Canal. The Welland is part of the St. Lawrence/ Great Lakes Waterway, a network of canals and rivers that provides passage for cargo ships and tankers between the Great Lakes and the Atlantic Ocean.

TOWARD THE 21ST CENTURY

During the 1990s, the people of Canada and the United States may need to remind themselves of that cooperative effort in the St. Lawrence Valley as they work to deepen not just a river, but also a relationship. That relationship grows more crucial every day as advances in communication and transportation bring the people and economies of both countries even closer together.

Canada has vast reserves of fresh water and also energy resources such as oil and hydroelectric power. The United States provides an enormous market for Canadian products and factories to turn more Canadian raw materials into finished goods.

The combination of Canada's natural resources and the additional industrial output of the United States promises great benefits for both countries, but achieving these benefits will require cooperation and patience on both sides of the border. The more the people of Canada and the United States know about each other, the easier it will be.

This cartoon poster credits Prime Minister John A. Macdonald for saving Canada from being taken over by the United States.

Questions

1. What were the three goals of Prime Minister Macdonald's National Policy?
2. What obstacles stood in the way of the westward expansion of Canada?
3. In what ways did completion of the transcontinental railway affect the growth of Canada?
4. In what ways is Canada important to the United States? In what ways is the United States important to Canada?
5. WHAT DO YOU THINK? What changes in technology that were developed around the turn of the 20th century, helped to make life on the Canadian prairie less dangerous and farming there more profitable?

Japanese Canadians are loaded onto a truck in Slocan, British Columbia, for their trip to an internment camp.

SOME GOVERNMENT ACTIONS that may seem necessary at the time they are taken turn out to be tragic mistakes. The treatment of Japanese families by the governments of Canada and the United States during World War II is a good and sad example. While fighting for freedom overseas, the governments of both countries were denying it to many thousands of people at home.

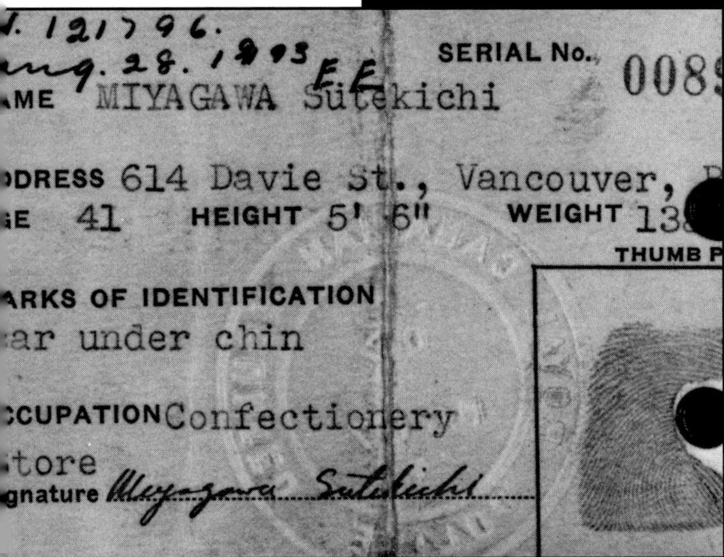

. 121796.
ug. 28. 1943 F.E.
SERIAL No. 008
ME MIYAGAWA Sutekichi
DRESS 614 Davie St., Vancouver,
E 41 HEIGHT 5' 6" WEIGHT 13
THUMB P
ARKS OF IDENTIFICATION
ar under chin
CUPATION Confectionery
tore
gnature Miyagawa Sutekichi

The internment identification card of Sutekichi Miyagawa, issued by the Canadian government, March 12, 1941.

Most Japanese and Chinese immigrants to Canada settled in coastal British Columbia where their neighbors were mainly white. They had long been the least welcome of Canada's many immigrant groups, but Japan's 1941 attack on the American Naval base at Pearl Harbor, Hawaii raised the level of prejudice against Japanese Canadians to new heights. Within two months, Canada's government had issued an order requiring all Japanese Canadians to leave the coastal area. Twenty-two thousand men, women and children were relocated to the interior of British Columbia and to other provinces. Most were housed in internment camps

A drawing of the Little River internment camp in New Brunswick, 1940.

that were hastily constructed dormitories clustered together in the wilderness and surrounded by barbed wire and armed guards.

Some people excused the practice as a wartime emergency measure designed to prevent Japanese Canadians from possibly interfering with the war effort out of loyality to their native land. But other people expressed shock and dismay at the sight of women and children being torn from their homes and treated like prisoners in a country that had so long prided itself on being a defender of freedom. Japanese Americans in the United States were treated in similar fashion. More than 40 years later, both countries formally apologized to those who had been interned during the war and to their families.

Bearer, whose photograph and specimen of signat
ar hereon, has been duly registered in compliance w
provisions of Order-in-Council P. C. 117.
ouver
Date) March 12 1941.
JAPANESE NATIONAL
INSPECTOR R.C.M.P.

A Sad Chapter

UNIT 3

A COUNTRY DIVIDED BY GEOGRAPHY

The people of Canada have much in common with the people of the United States. Both countries, for example, are nations of immigrants. But Canadians and Americans are different in many ways. Differences in geography and history create differences in people, too.

The geography that separates and defines Canada's natural regions also separates its people. In some ways, the various regions of Canada are like countries unto themselves. Each has a history, economy and culture that is different from those of the others.

Only since the middle of this century have advances in transportation and telecommunications begun to break down some of the natural walls that have long divided the people of Canada.

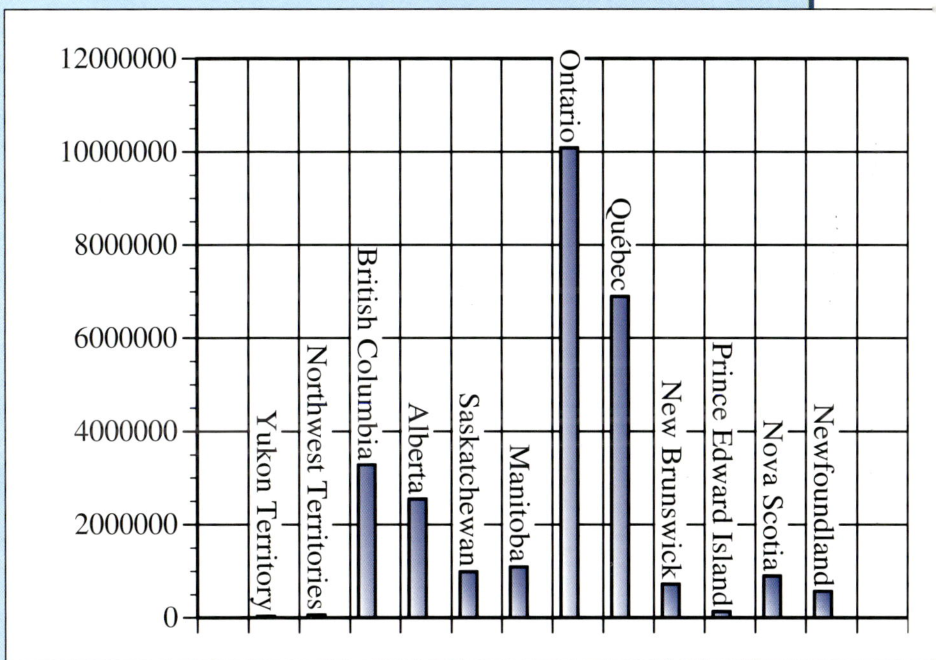

populations of the provinces and territories

ESSAY

A Nation of Immigrants

More than 29 million people live in Canada today. Fewer than a million of them are direct descendents of the original inhabitants, or Native peoples. The rest are immigrants or descendents of immigrants from all over the world.

No single group of Canadians represents more than half of the country's population. But people of British ancestry form the largest group—about 40 percent. The large size of this group reflects Canada's long history as a collection of English colonies. French Canadians are the next largest group, about 25 percent of the population. Their numbers reflect the fact that much of Canada was also a French colony for more than 150 years.

More recent immigrants to Canada have come from many other places in the world, including Asia, Africa, Central Europe and the Caribbean. Thus, Canadians today are a people of many colors, languages and religions. It is not unusual for students living in the country's largest cities to hear more than a dozen languages spoken in the hallways of their schools.

Immigrants living in Canada have experienced opportunities and prejudices similar to those living in the United States. Still, the immigrant experience in Canada has been different in at least one important way. The **melting pot** idea, which encourages immigrants to become like everyone else in their adopted country, did not take root in Canada to the same degree that it did during the early days of immigration in the United States. Instead of a melting pot, Canada became a **cultural mosaic**, a collection of cultures that main-

These immigrants are waiting to go ashore at Quebec City around 1911. Their clothing suggests that they may have been successful business people.

tain and even celebrate their differences under the flag of Canada. The government policy that supports the ideal of a cutural mosaic in Canada is called **multiculturalism**. Recently, many Americans have been asking their government to adopt a similar policy in the United States.

The recent increase in immigration from Asia has changed the face of many Canadian cities, especially Vancouver and Toronto, above.

The fact that Canada's Native peoples were joined by settlers from both France and England forced Canadians to live with cultural differences at an early point in their history. The Quebec Act, 1774, which gave French Canadians the legal right to maintain their language and culture, set an important example of tolerance that generations of Canadians have tried to practice with immigrants from other cultures.

Living with other cultures and languages, however, has always been a challenge, not only in Canada, but also all over the world. Getting along with people who are different requires a level of tolerance and understanding that some people are unable, or unwilling, to reach. Still, over the years, Canada has earned a reputation for trying to live up to the ideal that people can live together without being alike.

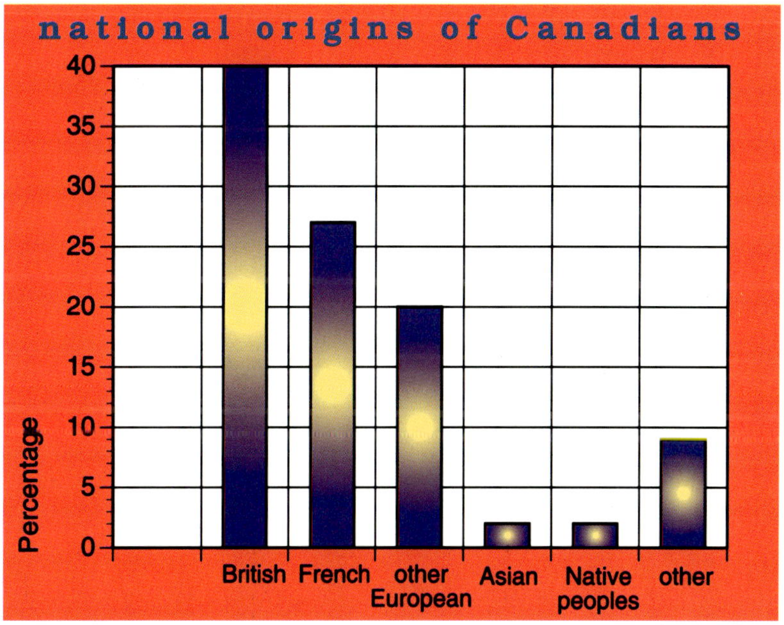

Whatever their ancestry, 80 percent of Canadians have settled within 100 miles of the Canada-United States border. About half live in either Quebec or Ontario. And even though Canada is famous for its mountains and forests, three out of four Canadians live in cities. Toronto, Montreal and Vancouver alone are home for about a third of all Canadians.

■

CHAPTER 8

Life in the Provinces of Eastern Canada

A fisherman hangs his catch out to dry.

TO GUIDE YOUR READING
Look for answers to these questions

1. What problems face the people who live in the provinces of Atlantic Canada?
2. In what ways are the people of Quebec and Ontario different from each other?

   In what ways are they similar?
3. How has recent immigration changed both Montreal and Toronto?
4. In what ways is Toronto important to the rest of Canada?
5. What challenges face cities that have many ethnic groups living side by side?

INTRODUCTION

Two-thirds of all Canadians live in the part of their country that extends from the Atlantic Ocean to the edge of the Canadian Shield. It is an area of great contrasts. Quaint fishing villages and small farming and mining communities share the landscape with strikingly modern cities. The centers of both English- and French-Canadian culture are also located in eastern Canada.

***Rural** life in the fishing villages, farm regions and mining communities has always been traditional and family centered. Today that way of life is undergoing drastic change. So is **urban** life in Canada's two largest cities, Toronto and Montreal. Once almost entirely English and French, the two cities are now home for millions of recent arrivals from all over the world.*

THE ATLANTIC PROVINCES

Life in Atlantic Canada is shaped by the sea. Almost all of the region's two million people live with familiar ocean sounds of crashing surf, squawking gulls and the haunting tones of distant foghorns.

Newfoundland is the most remote of the four provinces that make up this region of Canada. Only half of the province, called **Labrador**, is part of the Canadian mainland. The other half, where most Newfoundlanders live, is a rocky island about the size of Tennessee. Here, dense fog can blanket the coast for days. Sometimes the fog gets so thick that airports are forced to close and the ferry-boats that connect the island to the mainland must remain tied to their docks. During some months, a blind venture out to sea would be too dangerous because of the huge icebergs that lumber through the coastal waters. An iceberg off the coast of Newfoundland sank the huge passenger ship *Titanic* in 1912.

Prince Edward Island, New Brunswick and Nova Scotia are the other provinces that make up Atlantic Canada. For centuries, life in these provinces has revolved around fishing, farming and mining. Many of the weathered dwellings that line the coastal areas of Atlantic Canada have served as home for many generations of the same family. Often, three generations lived under the same roof at the same time. In many families, grandparents, parents and children worked side by side in the same workplace.

Because of the small size of their communities and the harshness of their daily lives, the people of Atlantic Canada have developed strong family and community ties. Most residents are small-town folk who know the names of their neighbors and local business people. Churches still play an important role in most towns and villages. Weddings and funerals are often community events.

Evidence of the region's first French settlers remains strong. In New Brunswick, people of

Wood from the hillsides of Atlantic Canada was used to build everything a fishing family needed: houses, docks, boats and lobster traps. Until the recent crisis in the fishing industry, life in the Atlantic fisheries remained virtually unchanged for many generations.

Nova Scotians of Scottish descent continue to celebrate their heritage.

Icebergs off the coast of Newfoundland. Only about 1/8 of each enormous ice block is visible above the water—the "tip of the iceberg."

French ancestry make up nearly a third of the population. But, today most people who live in Atlantic Canada speak English, some with a distinctive accent passed down from the region's Irish and Scott settlers. Canadians of African descent also live in the region, especially in and around Halifax, Nova Scotia. Many of their ancestors arrived from the United States by way of the Underground Railroad in the days before the American Civil War. Others came from British and French colonies in the Caribbean.

Each of the Atlantic provinces has at least one important port city: **Saint John's** in Newfoundland, **Charlottetown** in Prince Edward Island, **Saint John** in New Brunswick and **Halifax** in Nova Scotia. All four cities, though quite small compared to places like Toronto and Montreal, are modern commercial, business and entertainment centers. And they are all popular summer vacation destinations for travelers attracted by their historical sites, ocean scenery and delicious seafood.

For all of its scenic beauty, however, Atlantic Canada has long been one of the poorest regions in the country. Wages for the unskilled labor required by the industries that have traditionally been the backbone of its economy are usually quite low. Products from other parts of Canada are more expensive in Atlantic Canada because of high transportation costs. The region's economic woes have only gotten worse during the 1990s.

Labrador Sea
Goose Bay
NEWFOUNDLAND
St. John's
Grand Banks
Gulf of St. Lawrence
St. Lawrence River
PRINCE EDWARD ISLAND
Charlottetown
Sydney
NEW BRUNSWICK
NOVA SCOTIA
Fredericton
Saint John
Halifax
Quebec
Montreal
Ottawa
Toronto
Lake Ontario
Atlantic CANADA
500 km
0
500 Miles
provincial capital
national capital

A replica of the Bluenose, Canada's most famous sailing vessel, makes its way into Halifax harbor. The original schooner won many international sailing competitions in the 1920s and 1930s, but it was sold to a trading company in 1942. It sank near Haiti in 1946.

The Atlantic fisheries are almost fished out. For the first time in history, the government of Canada was forced to ban cod fishing in 1992 for a three-year period. It did so to give the fish a chance to increase their numbers. Thousands of people lost their jobs, and it is hard to tell how many will ever work in the fisheries again.

The coal-mining industry has also fallen on hard times. Due to lower demand for this smoky fuel, coal mines and processing plants all over the region have closed, forcing even more Atlantic Canadians to look for different jobs.

One ray of hope for the unemployed may be the recent discovery of huge pools of oil beneath the ocean floor just off the southeast coast of Newfoundland. Development of the **Hibernia Oil Field** would create a large number of jobs in the oil industry. Preliminary work on the project during the early 1990s provided nearly 4,000 jobs. But it is unclear when, or even if, Hibernia will be completed. Because of concerns over possible serious damage to the environment, Canada may decide to leave the oil right where it is.

St. John's, Newfoundland.

Canadian author Lucy Maud Montgomery made Prince Edward Island famous in 1908 with her book Anne of Green Gables. The story was so popular that Ms. Montgomery wrote a series of books about the little girl with bright red hair who lived in the lovely green-gabled house on Prince Edward Island.

Anne of Green Gables

QUEBEC: HEARTLAND OF FRENCH CANADA

Quebec is the largest province in Canada. Although it is the center of French-Canadian culture, people of many other cultures and language groups also live there. No other part of Canada reflects its complicated history better than Quebec.

Larger in size than most countries, Quebec is thinly populated except for its southernmost portion. The vast majority of its people live in the St. Lawrence and Ottawa river valleys. Some live on the many narrow farm lots that have lined these rivers for hundreds of years. Most people, however, live in Montreal, Quebec City, or one of the province's few smaller cities.

Large groups of Canada's Native peoples live in Quebec. In the northern part, the **Inuit** inhabit a barren and snowy landscape, far away from most of the province's French and English inhabitants. Some still live as their ancestors did 15,000 years ago.

In southern Quebec, descendents of North American Native peoples make their homes on **reserves**. On these tracts of land, residents live removed

These two boys live in northern Quebec. Their ancestors were among the first people to settle in North America about 15,000 years ago.

from the laws and culture of the rest of Canada. Several of the reserves extend into the United States, a reminder of the days before European settlers divided the land with man-made boundaries. As in the North, Native traditions on the reserves have been kept alive for many thousands of years.

RURAL QUEBEC

In addition to its few cities, southern Quebec is dotted with hundreds of picturesque towns and villages. Almost every one is shadowed by the tall silver steeple of a Roman Catholic church. Once at the very center of life in New France, the Catholic church has continued to play an important role in the lives of most French-speaking people in Quebec, especially those who live in the rural areas.

The church's influence is reflected in the names of the provinces towns and villages. Most are named after a Roman Catholic saint. The birthday of Saint John the Baptist, June 24, is celebrated as a provincial holiday.

Family farms line both the St Lawrence and Ottawa rivers from one end to the other. Some of the farms have been in the same family for more than 200 years. They sit on some of the most fertile soil in the world. The landscape is as flat as a pancake–it was once the floor of an inland sea.

Most people in rural Quebec still live in small wood and stone houses. Perched on top of their steep roofs, stone chimneys carry sweet-smelling wood smoke from stoves and fireplaces below. The French language is everywhere. More than 80 percent of the people speak it and provincial laws require almost all outdoor signs in Quebec to be written in French.

Although modern satellite dishes, snowmobiles and powerboats can be seen beside many homes, life is still traditional and family-centered. Winter sports are popular, especially skiing, skating, sledding and (the favorite) ice hockey. The food is hearty. Rich vegetable soups, meat pies, farm-fresh butter and other dairy products, along with sweet maple desserts, are popular, locally produced foods. They taste their best when enjoyed near a warm wood fire on a cold winter day.

From the earliest days, farm lots along the St. Lawrence and other rivers were made long and narrow to give every farmer frontage on the river.

The skyline of almost every town and village in rural Quebec is dominated by the silver steeple of at least one Roman Catholic church.

The snowmobile was invented in Quebec in 1937 by J. Armand Bombardier. Riding the power sleds is now a popular sport almost everywhere in the world where snow falls.

MONTREAL

Though little more than a dot on the map of Quebec, Montreal is home for nearly half of all the people in the province. The city itself sits on an island in the St. Lawrence River. In the center of the island, **Mount Royal**, the only mountain for 30 miles around, forms a backdrop for the city's modern skyline.

Montreal offers a stark contrast of old and new. The city's 350-year history is reflected in many of its neighborhoods. In a restored waterfront area called Old Montreal, visitors can journey back in time down cobblestone streets in horse-drawn carriages. Montreal also features exciting modern architecture, excellent theater, art galleries, museums, professional sports and some of the finest restaurants in the world. It is also the provincial center of business and banking.

There is more to Montreal than what appears on the surface. Beneath the downtown streets is another busy world of underground shops, movie theatres and restaurants. All are connected by walkways, escalators and gleaming subway trains that whiz by almost silently on fat rubber tires. Above ground or below, Montreal is safe, clean and

Visitors to Old Montreal travel cobblestone streets that are lined with old stone and brick buildings. Some of the buildings are nearly 350 years old.

Montreal's downtown center contrasts the very old and the very new.

always lively. No wonder it is such a favorite destination for tourists from around the world, especially from the United States.

For most of its history, Montreal was almost exclusively French, with some English. Although 70 percent of Montreal's population is still French-speaking, immigration during this century, especially during the last 40 years, has changed the face of the city. People of French ancestry are still the largest single group living in Montreal, but dozens of other ethnic groups now contribute to its international flavor.

Montreal is proud of its lively "Chinatown," located downtown, and "Little Italy," situated north of the city center. Several hundred thousand people of Italian, Portuguese, Greek and Eastern European ancestry live in the many distinctive neighborhoods that line the eastern base of Mount Royal. Montreal is also the adopted home for large numbers of people of African, Asian, Indian and Latin American descent. The **diversity** of language, food, fashion, music and art that results from this rich mix of cultures helps make Montreal one of the most exciting cities in the world.

In the fascinating underground world beneath the streets of Montreal, restaurants, shops, banks and movie theaters are linked by the speedy trains of the Metro.

One of the Metro's modern and clean stations.

OTHER CITIES IN QUEBEC

The jolly snowman Bonhomme is the mascot of the Quebec Winter Carnival, an annual weeklong celebration of winter that is often referred to as "Mardi Gras North."

Unlike Montreal, Quebec's other, much smaller cities are almost exclusively French.

Quebec City is the oldest city and port in Canada. It is also the capital of the province. Perched high on a sheer cliff above the St. Lawrence River, it too is a popular tourist attraction. Like Montreal, Quebec City is a fascinating mix of the very old and the very new. Narrow cobblestone streets and stone buildings, some nearly 400 years old, alternate with tall glass skyscrapers and modern hotels.

Some of the oldest buildings in Quebec City are found along the river at the base of the cliff in what has long been referred to as Lower Town. This is where Samuel de Champlain built the first permanent French settlement on the St. Lawrence in 1608. As it grew, most new residents settled on top of the cliff where there was more room and also a better view of the river. That view was important to their survival because Quebec City remained under constant threat of attack by the English during its first 150 years. Its residents turned tiny Quebec into a fortress by surrounding the clifftop portion of the settlement with high stone walls lined with cannons. It is the only completely walled city ever built in North America.

Part of the wall surrounding Quebec City is visible just behind the brightly colored rooftops of the houses below.

Nestled in the Appalachian mountains near the Vermont border, **Sherbrooke** is Quebec's third largest city. Founded two centuries ago by a small group of loyalists from the United States, the city today is mostly French speaking. Sherbrooke boasts many thriving textile and clothing factories, a large university and a beautiful natural setting.

Hull sits on the banks of the Ottawa River directly across from the city of Ottawa, Ontario. The graceful bridges that connect Hull with its sister city in the National Capital Region are anchored in the same rocky bluff that supports the huge stone buildings of the Canadian Parliament. The bridges speed traffic between the two cities and are a symbolic link between Canada's two official founding peoples.

An ice castle at the Quebec Winter Carnival, held each February in Quebec City.

ONTARIO: HEARTLAND OF ENGLISH CANADA

Ontario is Canada's second-largest province and, like Quebec, has more territory than most countries. Ontario is the heartland of English Canada, having been founded as a home for loyalists who decided not to take part in the American Revolution. They were soon joined by thousands of other Americans attracted by the region's excellent farmland. Later, Ontario's population changed with the addition of more than 40,000 African Americans seeking freedom from slavery in the United States. They came at about the same time as a flood of Irish people who had been forced from their homeland by a long and terrible famine.

Evidence of Canada's British colonial past can be found almost everywhere in the province. Many of Ontario's cities, such as Windsor, Guelph and London, are named after cities or towns in Great Britain. And their street names represent almost everyone who was ever a member of the British royal family.

The vast majority of Ontarians live in the southern part of the province, surrounded on three sides by the United States. Most can drive to a large American city, such as Buffalo or Detroit, in a matter of hours, or less. For almost everyone living in Ontario, contact with an American city is as close as the nearest television. It is fair to say that most people who live in Ontario have more contact with Americans than with the people who live in the other provinces of their own country.

A family farm in the St. Lawrence Lowlands Region of southern Ontario. The home is near the barns that shelter a variety of animals including cows, chickens, horses and sometimes hogs. One of the barns contains the farm machinery that is used to plant and harvest the many acres of land owned by the family.

RURAL ONTARIO

Agriculture in southern Ontario benefits from the rich soil of the Great Lakes Lowlands and a growing season of about five months. No wonder it is Canada's most productive agricultural region. While large, mechanized factory farms produce most of Ontario's food products, thousands of smaller family farms still survive.

Life on these farms involves hard work for every member of the family. From sunrise to sunset, especially during the growing season, much effort is required to get from the land all it can give. Even with the help of modern machinery, farm chores such as caring for animals, milking cows, planting seed, harvesting grains, picking fruits and vegetables and repairing equipment, is time-consuming and tiring. Then there is the task of preparing the food for market and storing it for the winter.

The long hours of work leave little opportunity for socializing, but rural Ontarians make time to enjoy community suppers and dances where country-and-western music and square dancing are also popular. Some of the province's country musicians have become international stars.

TORONTO

The great majority of the people of Ontario live in its many busy cities. Most are located along Highway 401, one of the most heavily traveled highways in North America. Like a paved version of Quebec's St. Lawrence River, the highway stitches together Ontario's far-flung population centers from Windsor to Cornwall. It is busiest in and around Toronto, Canada's largest city, where it is often clogged with miles of eight-lane bumper-to-bumper traffic.

Located on the western shore of Lake Ontario, Toronto is the capital of Ontario. While Montreal's charm is rooted in a past that dates back to the early 1600s, Toronto is one of most modern cities in North America. Most of its buildings were constructed during the 20th century and many of them, especially those along the waterfront that form Toronto's futuristic skyline, were built during the last 30 years. Among them is the world's tallest freestanding structure, the awesome 110 story CN Tower.

Built to loft powerful radio and telecommunications antennas high into the sky, the skinny cement tower also supports a doughnut-shaped revolving restaurant that is so high that diners look *down* on airplanes headed to and from Toronto's busy airports. Even farther up the tower, a tiny observation deck provides a more than 100-mile panorama for those daring enough to brave its eerie heights. Both restaurant and observation deck are served by speedy elevators that race up and down the tower just inside long narrow windows.

The CN Tower is the tallest freestanding structure in the world.

At the base of the tower, Toronto's sparkling **SkyDome** also adds to the waterfront's 21st century look. The huge stadium is the home of the Toronto Blue Jays baseball team. Games and other special events in the "SkyDome" are held rain or shine, summer or winter. The playing field is protected by a mechanical roof that can be closed in just 20 minutes. When the roof is open, players must be careful not to be distracted by the spectacular view of the CN tower piercing the sky like a Starwars spaceship.

Like Montreal, Toronto has a sprawling underground city. It is a brightly lit world of offices, restaurants, theaters and shops, all connected by fast moving escalators and modern subway trains.

Toronto is the financial and communications center of Canada. Many of the gleaming skyscrapers in the downtown area are headquarters for important Canadian banks, insurance companies and other financial institutions, including the

The SkyDome has a retractable roof so that the Blue Jays can play baseball no matter how bad the weather may be outside.

Toronto Stock Exchange. Also based in Toronto are the headquarters for Canada's two English-language radio and television networks, most of the country's English magazine and book publishers and the *Globe and Mail*, often referred to as Canada's national newspaper.

The power and influence exerted by Toronto have long been resented by people in other parts of Canada. Still, Toronto's lure has proven irresistible. The city and its suburbs are home for some four million people—nearly one out of every seven Canadians!

Just blocks away from Toronto's waterfront skyscrapers, the remainder of the city is largely a collection of single-family homes and apartment houses that form tidy neighborhoods, each with its unique character.

Toronto, like Montreal, has a rich ethnic mix. As they have in many other North American cities, people of similar ethnic background have tended to cluster together in separate neighborhoods after arriving from their homeland. It is only natural for people living in a strange new country to seek out neighbors who speak the same language or attend the same church.

This 1959 cartoon pokes fun at Toronto's powerful role in shaping Canada's national identity.

The head offices of many of Canada's important banks, insurance companies, international corporations, and the country's largest stock exchange, are located inside these skyscrapers in downtown Toronto.

Once almost exclusively English, Toronto today is a city of many nationalities. Large groups of Chinese and Vietnamese people have settled side by side in a large area located only a few blocks from the city's waterfront skyscrapers.

A tour of these neighborhoods is like a visit to Greece, Portugal, Italy, the West Indies and China, all rolled into one. The rapid changes in architecture, language, clothing and food encountered during a trip across the city make Toronto a fascinating and exciting place to live and to visit.

However interesting it may be, Toronto's multicultural character creates special challenges for all of its citizens. The danger of conflict between people of different cultures is always present. Misunderstandings between different culture groups are always difficult to resolve, especially when different languages are involved. Because it is home to so many cultures so closely packed together, Toronto's challenge is clear.

The city government has taken steps to help newcomers feel welcome. Water bills, for example, are prepared in six different languages, and ethnic festivals and parades are supported. Local radio and television stations broadcast in dozens of languages day and night.

CLOCKWISE from above

• In addition to lively local theater, popular plays from London and New York are staged in Toronto with a scale and quality equal to the original productions—like this presentation of the epic musical Miss Saigon.

• The Toronto Maple Leafs hockey team is one of the oldest franchises in the NHL.

• Since the early 1990s, tickets for almost every Blue Jays game have been sold out. The Jays won back-to-back World Series championships in 1992 and 1993.

• International fairs, like this celebration of Caribbean culture, are an important part of life in Toronto.

Toronto

Even with the rapid growth and increasing importance of other Canadian cities such as Edmonton, Calgary and Vancouver, Toronto remains at the center of English-Canadian culture. It is probably the Canadian city most influenced by American culture because it is located near so many large American cities.

Members of the Black Watch with their oversized fuzzy helmets are a familiar sight on Parliament Hill in Ottawa. They are a ceremonial reminder of the many traditions that Canada imported from Great Britain.

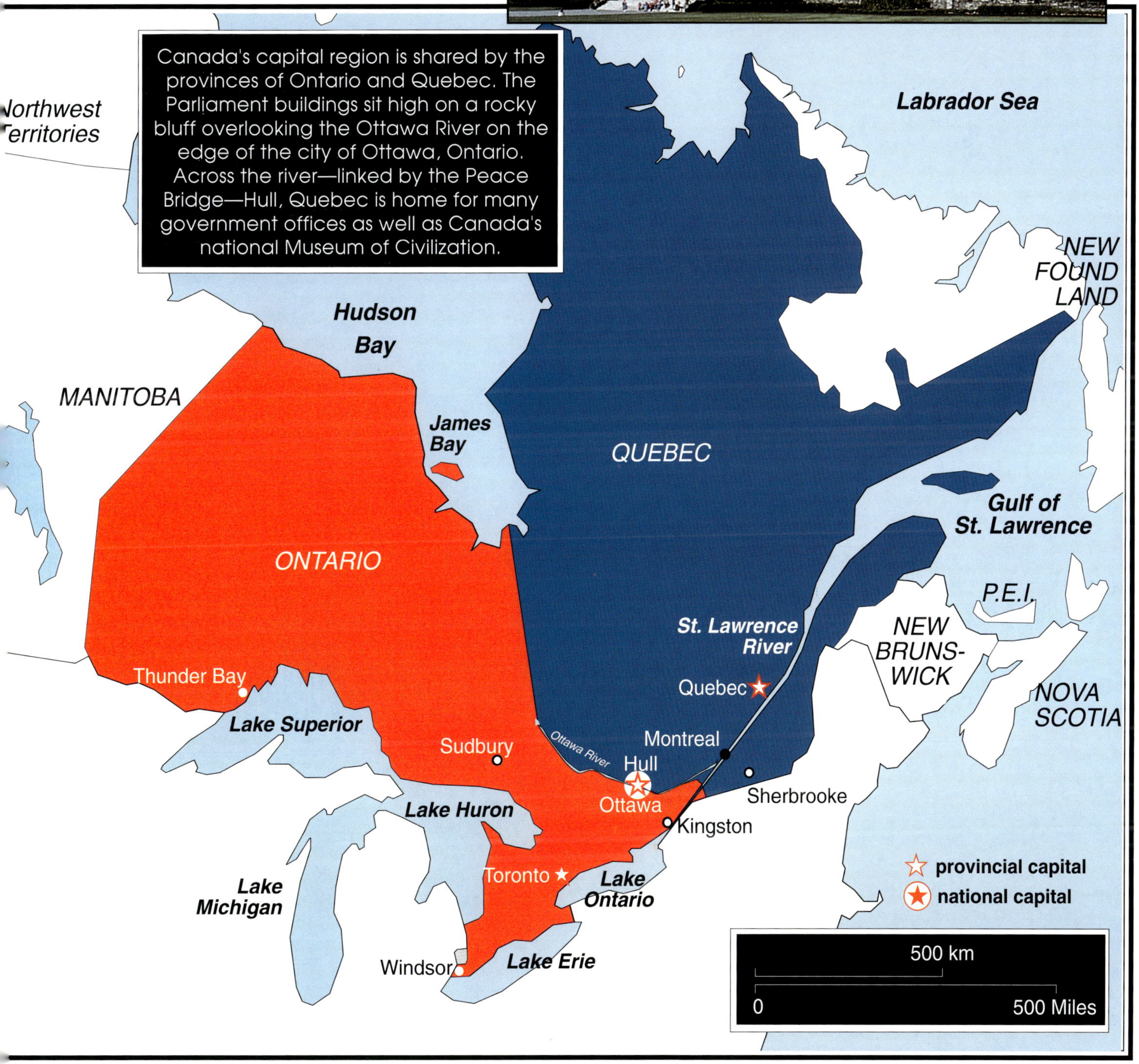

Canada's capital region is shared by the provinces of Ontario and Quebec. The Parliament buildings sit high on a rocky bluff overlooking the Ottawa River on the edge of the city of Ottawa, Ontario. Across the river—linked by the Peace Bridge—Hull, Quebec is home for many government offices as well as Canada's national Museum of Civilization.

Tulips thrive in the warm spring breezes along the Rideau Canal in Ottawa. The Netherlands sends the bulbs to Canada each year in appreciation for Canada's help during World War II.

Skaters take to the ice on the Rideau Canal near the Parliament Buildings in Ottawa—"Wait a minute, wasn't that the Prime Minister skating by on the way to work?"

OTTAWA: THE CAPITAL OF CANADA

Ottawa is Canada's national capital. A large percentage of its population is employed by the government as secretaries, file clerks, office managers, computer operators, judges, lawyers and accountants.

So far, Ottawa has managed to maintain much of its original small-town charm while becoming one of Canada's fastest growing urban centers. Visitors to the National Capital Region of Ottawa-Hull are struck by the cleanliness and beauty of the downtown area, which features historic government buildings and impressive museums, libraries and galleries. The scenic Rideau Canal and Waterway, which connects the Ottawa and St. Lawrence rivers, runs through the heart of Ottawa and into the suburbs. It is crowded with pleasure boats during the summer months and skaters during the winter. Just south of the downtown area, the canal is lined with majestic stone homes which are surrounded by huge rolling lawns, colorful gardens and towering trees.

In the spring, Ottawa glows with the colors of hundreds of thousands of brilliantly colored tulips. The flowers were a thank-you gift from the people of the Netherlands for Canada's help during World War II.

The Musée canadien des civilisations/Canadian Museum of Civilization is located in Hull, Quebec, directly across the Ottawa River from the Parliament Buildings (which are visible in the background of this photo). The museum's elaborate exhibits trace the history of civilization in Canada from its earliest days.

Sudbury, Ontario, is home to the main plant of Inco, one of Canada's largest mining companies. The plant's towering smokestacks are city landmarks. One of the stacks is the tallest in the world.

Questions

1. Why are the Atlantic provinces today the poorest provinces in all of Canada?
2. In what ways is Montreal the most important city in the province of Quebec?
3. What are the largest immigrant groups living in Toronto and Montreal?
4. List 4 reasons why Toronto is often referred to as the most important city in Canada?
5. WHAT DO YOU THINK? Rivalries between Montreal and Toronto in professional sports have always been more intense than those between any other cities in Canada. Why?

CHAPTER 9

Life in the Prairie Provinces

On reserves across western Canada, descendants of the prairie's earliest inhabitants keep their culture alive.

TO GUIDE YOUR READING
Look for answers to these questions

1. How are the people who live in the prairie provinces different from the people who live in eastern Canada?
2. Why is farming on the prairie such a challenge?
3. What three important cities are located on the prairie and why are they important to Canada?
4. What changes in transportation and technology are helping to bring the people of eastern and western Canada closer together?

INTRODUCTION

For more than 200 years, the Canadian Shield has been as much a barrier to Canadian unity as different languages and cultures. Like a huge wall, its rock and its forests divide Canada into east and west.

The cities of western Canada were little more than tiny settlements or forts as recently as 100 years ago. Then the railway came, and families began to settle on the free land offered by the Canadian government and the railway companies.

Life on the prairie has always centered on growing grain and raising cattle. During the last 50 years, manufacturing, oil and natural gas industries have brought new prosperity to western Canada, especially to its cities and towns.

Because they live so far away from the political, financial and media capitals of eastern Canada, western Canadians have often complained of feeling left out of the important affairs of their country. Many people believe, however, that faster and better transportation and communications will now bring eastern and western Canadians closer together.

PEOPLE OF THE PRAIRIE

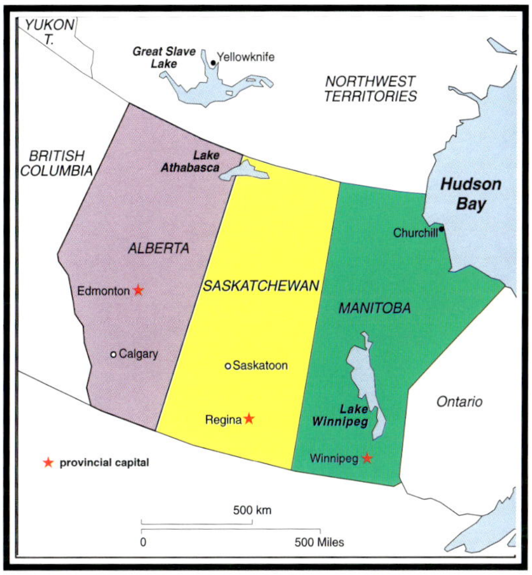

Extending from the edge of the Canadian Shield to the base of the Canadian Rockies, the prairie provinces of **Manitoba**, **Saskatchewan** and **Alberta** are home to nearly four million Canadians. Many are the grandchildren of families that were drawn to the so-called "last, best West" by offers of free land from the Canadian government during the early 20th century. Some came from eastern Canada, the United States and Great Britain. Others came from Norway, Ireland and Russia. Almost all of the new arrivals were white, but they were not all alike. A distinct language, religion and set of customs gave each group its own place in the Canadian mosaic.

Ukrainians were one of the largest groups to settle in the West. They clustered together, mostly in Manitoba and Saskatchewan. The onion-shaped spires of their Eastern Orthodox Churches are among the most easily recognized landmarks on the prairie.

A typically large prairie farmstead. The nearest neighbors are more than a mile away.

Many Native tribes have lived on the prairie for some 10,000 years. Their culture and influence can be seen and felt across western Canada. Some have traded their traditional dress for business suits or cowboy boots and have moved to a town or city. Others remain on one of the several reserves found in western Canada. Here, though their lives have been changed by video technology and modern conveniences, they struggle to keep their culture alive.

THE CHALLENGE OF PRAIRIE LIFE

Almost all prairie life is connected in some way to farming, ranching or oil, even in the cities. Life on the open prairie is harsh and risky, especially for farmers. Months of hard work can be wiped out in less than a day by weather that can be as brutal as it is unpredictable. The peacefulness of a warm autumn day may suddenly be broken by a plunge in temperature accompanied by powerful winds and pounding hail that can turn a lush field of grain into a flat, frozen wasteland in less than an hour.

During the winter, frigid temperatures and howling winds can combine to freeze unprotected skin

The Ukrainian Catholic Church at Angle Lake, Alberta. Churches like this one, topped by an onion-shaped dome, are a familiar sight on the prairie.

in a matter of minutes. Summer droughts, tornados and violent thunderstorms are other prairie risks. No wonder that farmers make sure to keep up with their local weather forecasts all day long.

The prairie appears to go on forever.

In addition to the extremes of weather, life on the prairie is shaped by the openness and flatness of the landscape. The view from almost anywhere is unbroken clear to the horizon. The prairie sky is wonderful to behold. It surrounds the viewer like a huge, brightly painted dome, magnifying the beauty of a sunset or a starry night.

Unlike most of the farms in eastern Canada, prairie farms are very large. The average size is over 1,000 acres. Thus, most farm families on the prairie live miles from their nearest neighbors or town. Out of necessity, families are closely knit. Family members must work together to survive and there is often little social life. Many people who live on prairie farms would not trade their quiet, family-centered privacy for anything, but many others find the same life lonely and even depressing.

New landmarks on the prairie, oil wells, have brought prosperity to parts of western Canada.

RANCHES AND OIL WELLS

Not all of the prairie is covered with grain. The landscapes of both Alberta and western Saskatchewan are dotted with wells that pump oil and natural gas. Huge pipelines carry both fuels across Canada and into the United States.

The southern prairie contains most of Canada's cattle ranches. Like prairie farms, these can be large in size. Life in and near Canada's oil and cattle towns may be lonely sometimes, but it is seldom boring. Like their counterparts in the western United States, western Canadians enjoy a rugged outdoor life filled with horses, cattle drives, pick-up trucks, country music, outdoor barbecues and rodeos.

Many of the people who live in the region's cattle towns and ranches are descendants of the Americans who moved into the area from the neighboring Great Plains during the late 1800s. At that time, the Canada-United States border west of the Great Lakes was virtually unknown by anyone but

mapmakers and government officials. Most settled in what is today southern Alberta, where cowhands on horseback still ride herd on thousands of well-fed beef cattle against the spectacular backdrop of the snow-peaked Canadian Rockies. Because of its mix of horses and oil wells, Alberta is often referred to as the Texas of Canada.

Cattle ranches line much of the Canada-United States border in western Canada, especially in Alberta and Saskatchewan.

Alberta's and Saskatchewan's reserves of oil and natural gas have brought rapid change and new prosperity to western Canada. The importance of these resources, and the wealth they bring, has given westerners new power and influence in dealing with the rest of Canada.

CITIES OF THE PRAIRIE

Although the prairie landscape is dominated by miles and miles of flat farmland, most people who live in the region today live in a city.

Winnipeg is the capital of and largest city in the province of Manitoba. It is the home of half of the province's people. Since the railway arrived in

1885, Winnipeg has prospered in its role as Canada's Gateway to the West. The city grew rapidly during the early years of the 20th century serving as the jumping-off point for the tide of European immigrants who were headed for the open prairie. A good number of them, however, settled in one of Winnipeg's many ethnic neighborhoods where their descendants continue to look forward to the annual Folklorama. The week-long event brings thousands of residents and tourists to the city streets to celebrate their international roots.

Edmonton is the largest city in Alberta and is the capital of the province. Located in the center of the province on the northern stretch of the Saskatchewan River, it has long been known as the Gateway to the North. Its location has made it a favorite destination for many Albertans who have given up farming. Eastern Canadians looking for new jobs have also made their homes here.

There is evidence that, 5,000 years ago, Native people camped near where Edmonton stands today. A pair of competitive trading forts built by the Hudson's Bay Company and the Northwest Company, another fur trading company, in 1795 were the first permanent settlements. Once the

serious

center of the fur trade in western Canada, Edmonton is now the center of the country's oil and petrochemical industry. It is a city of beautiful river views, manicured green spaces and shining office towers.

Edmonton is considered by many to be the cultural capital of the Prairie Region. Its symphony orchestra, and opera and theater organizations are among the largest in Canada. The city also has a very active and visible community of painters, potters, poets, writers and filmmakers. Many are associated with the University of Alberta, which is located in Edmonton. Not yet 100 years old, the university is one of Canada's finest.

The city has recently become most famous as home of the **West Edmonton Mall**, the largest indoor shopping and entertainment complex in the world. The mall houses more than 800 stores, 110 food outlets, many movie theaters and a hotel for shoppers from across Canada and around the world. It has its own lake with sharks and submarines as well as a frozen skating rink and also the world's largest indoor amusement park, complete with a triple-loop rollercoaster that is 12 stories high.

m a l l !

The West Edmonton Mall is the largest shopping and entertainment complex in the world.

No matter how modern it has become, Calgary has remained true to its roots. The annual Calgary Stampede has attracted cowboys, cowgirls and tenderfoot tourists since 1912.

South of Edmonton, at base of the Rocky Mountains is Calgary, the fastest-growing city in the region. Like most other cities on the prairie, Calgary owes its existence to the railway. It, too, has enjoyed a recent prosperity fueled by the profits from nearby oil wells and natural gas.

During the 20th century, Calgary has been transformed from a lonely and dusty cattle town into a modern, exciting city that is well connected to the rest of the world. Although it is still a long way from the population centers of eastern Canada, distance means little in this age of telecommunications and speedy jet aircraft.

No matter how modern it has become, Calgary has remained true to its roots. The city's most popular event is an annual rodeo celebration known as the **Calgary Stampede**. The event draws spectators and participants from all over the world.

Once a dusty cattle town, Calgary, Alberta, is now one of the most beautiful and modern cities in North America; it is also one of the fastest growing.

American visitors to Calgary often compare the city to Dallas or Houston. Cowboy hats and western boots are seen everywhere, worn with everything from jeans to business suits. Calgary restaurants feature thick, juicy steaks, and country-and-western music stations fill the radio dial.

Calgary's indoor sports and entertainment arena, the **Saddledome,** is built in the shape of a saddle so huge that a horse big enough to wear it could probably leap over the rockies. Its reflection in the windows of nearby skyscrapers creates a picture worth a thousand words about what makes this city special.

Inside the Saddledome, fans cheer at indoor rodeos or root for their hockey team, protected from whatever weather may be waiting outside. ■

The Saddledome, Calgary's indoor sporting and exhibition arena, reflects this city's long attachment to horses and the people who ride them.

Questions

1. Describe three challenges faced by prairie farmers.
2. Why are railways so important to prairie farmers?
3. How did the discovery of oil in western Canada affect its relationship with eastern Canada?
4. Select one city in western Canada and explain why you would like to live there.
5. WHAT DO YOU THINK? In what ways is life in western Canada similar to life in the western United States?

CHAPTER 10

Final Frontiers: British Columbia and the North

A restored steam locomotive winds its way along the Fraser River through the spectacular beauty of the Canadian Rockies.

TO GUIDE YOUR READING
Look for answers to these questions

1. In what ways are British Columbia and the North Canada's final frontiers?
2. How have changes in technology allowed Vancouver to become one of Canada's most important and fastest-growing cities?
3. Why is the North so important to the future of Canada?
4. How has the Canadian government changed the lives of the Native peoples who live in the North?

INTRODUCTION

In western Alberta, the Canadian Rockies shoot up from the prairie floor like giant icebergs from the ocean—only much taller. Majestic and rugged, they create still another wall dividing the people of Canada.

The mountains cover western Alberta and extend across Canada's western-most province, British Columbia, reaching northward along the Pacific coast all the way to Alaska. To the east of Alaska, the Yukon and the Northwest Territories together with northern Quebec form Canada's flat, frozen rooftop, a region Canadians call the North.

Located so far from the country's early European settlements, both British Columbia and the North have been historically isolated from the heart of

Canadian life. During the last two decades, however, new technologies have begun to change the way eastern Canada views and deals with its two final frontiers.

BRITISH COLUMBIA: A SUCCESS STORY OF THE LATE 20th CENTURY

British Columbia is Canada's most rapidly growing province. Only Ontario and Quebec have populations larger than British Columbia's 3.3 million. The province shares two borders with the United States. It borders the states of Washington, Idaho and Montana in the south and Alaska in the northwest. Most British Columbians live in the southern-most portion of the province along the Fraser Delta.

Modern technology accounts for British Columbia's recent success and promises more for its future. Once isolated from the rest of Canada by the Rockies and from much of the rest of the world by the Pacific Ocean, the province was almost completely dependent on fishing, lumbering and mining. Today, affordable jet travel and telecommunications links allow British Columbia to take greater advantage of what is turning out to be its most valuable resource: spectacular natural beauty.

This rugged mountain face in the Rockies is sheer rock, with no soil or vegetation.

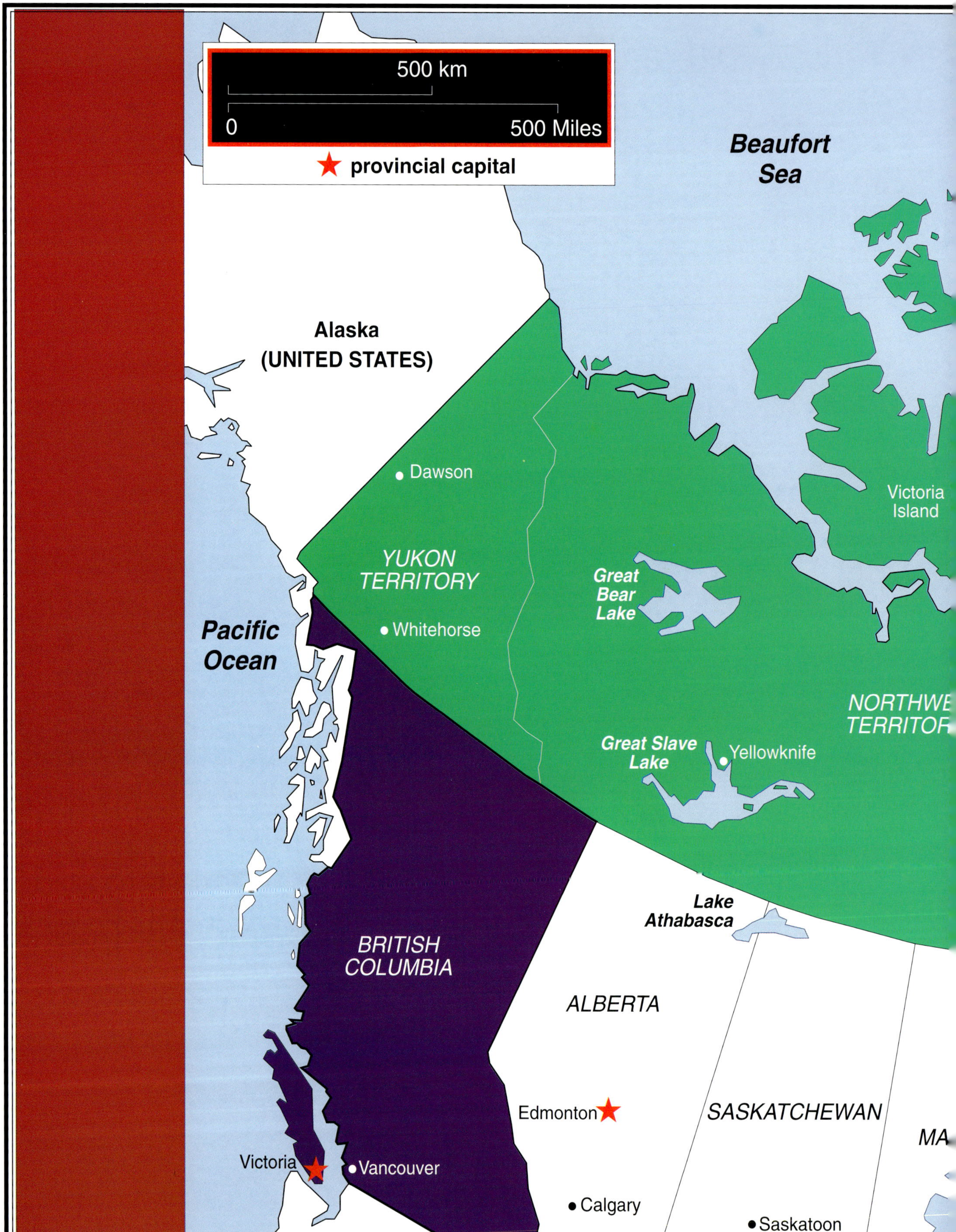
500 km
0
500 Miles
provincial capital
Beaufort Sea
Alaska (UNITED STATES)
Dawson
YUKON TERRITORY
Whitehorse
Victoria Island
Great Bear Lake
Pacific Ocean
Great Slave Lake
Yellowknife
Lake Athabasca
BRITISH COLUMBIA
ALBERTA
Edmonton
SASKATCHEWAN
Victoria
Vancouver
Calgary
Saskatoon

final frontiers

BRITISH COLUMBIA AND THE NORTH

Even as Vancouver has grown into one of the commercial and financial capitals of the world, the forest industry remains very important to the economy of British Columbia.

The province has become a popular tourist center and, due to the moderate climate of the British Columbia coast and Vancouver Island, it has also become a favorite place to retire. Many carefully planned retirement villages provide safety, quiet, recreation, entertainment and health-care for thousands of Canada's senior citizens.

International corporations looking for new bases of operations have also discovered British Columbia. Almost half of the province's trade is with **Pacific Rim nations**, nations that have a coastline on the Pacific Ocean, such as the United States, China, Japan, Korea and Vietnam.

OF TOURISTS AND LUMBER JACKS

The mountains and valleys of British Columbia, where some of the world's most breathtaking scenery and finest skiing are found, attract thousands of Canadian and international travelers to the region's many beautiful resorts and lodges.

The mountains are also home for many of the people connected to the important forest-products industry. Here, in logging towns and lumber camps, workers with strong muscles and powerful equipment begin the process of turning trees into the many wood and paper products which are sold across Canada and around the world.

Most jobs in the forest industry require hard, physical work and much of it is undertaken in wilderness areas far removed from many of the modern conveniences most people take for granted. But the good pay and the healthy appeal of working outdoors make logging and lumbering an attractive career choice for young Canadians willing to endure its hardships.

VANCOUVER IS CANADA'S WINDOW ON THE PACIFIC

As abruptly as they rise at the edge of the prairie, 500 miles farther west, the Rockies dive steeply towards the Pacific Ocean leaving only a thin strip of coastline at the water's edge. Close to the United States border and sandwiched between mountain and sea, the city of Vancouver thrives in its jeweled setting.

Pleasure boats fill marinas in Vancouver harbor against a backdrop of towering mountains and modern skyscrapers.

Vancouver is Canada's window on the Pacific. The culture of the city is greatly influenced by the beauty and bounty of the sea.

Vancouver is home for two out of every five British Columbians. Because it is separated from the rest of Canada by the great wall of the Rockies, most of Vancouver's business and culture has been more closely connected to the west coast of the United States and to Asia. The city is 350 miles closer to Japan than it is to Nova Scotia. Its population reflects its Pacific Rim location: a third of Vancouver school children speak either Japanese or Chinese as their first language. Other Asian people add to the rich ethnic mix. The city's many commercial ties with Pacific Rim nations have created thousands of jobs connected with international trade, banking and finance.

Residents of Vancouver, like those of the fishing villages and small cities of Atlantic Canada, enjoy the sights and sounds of the sea and the bounty of its harvest. But the southern coast of British Columbia is today much more prosperous than Atlantic Canada. Fishing, especially for salmon, remains an important industry and the city's markets and restaurants are famous for their glistening fresh seafood. The fishing boats in Vancouver harbor are greatly outnumbered by sleek yachts and colorful sailboats that, from a distance, appear as a flurry of bright confetti against the deep blue waters of the Pacific Ocean.

The city's moderate climate has influenced the design of its rapid transit system. Unlike the underground trains of Montreal and Toronto, Vancouver's futuristic SkyTrain weaves its way through the city skyline, high above crowded streets.

Vancouver is also the export harbor for more and more crops grown on the prairie. Mile-long trains made up of hundreds of boxcars brimming with golden grain from southern Saskatchewan and Alberta snake through mountain passes and long dark tunnels on their way to Vancouver. Here the grain is loaded onto huge freighters for delivery to nations along the Pacific Rim.

Ocean liners docked in Vancouver harbor. The city is a popular port for the cruise ships that travel up and down the Pacific coast from Alaska to Mexico, as well as for passenger and cargo ships that travel the Pacific Rim.

Native Peoples of the Pacific Coast

THE NATIVE PEOPLES OF CANADA'S Pacific coast were like no other in North America. Blessed with an incredible abundance of resources and a moderate—if a bit rainy—climate, they led a pleasant outdoor life in beautiful natural surroundings and enjoyed an ample, varied and delicious diet. Their's was a world of lush cedar forests, deep mountain valleys, blue Pacific waters and steeply walled inlets, called fiords. The ocean teemed with whales, halibut, otters and seal. Every low tide left rock and reef covered with tasty shellfish. The thick, green forest, nurtured by almost daily rainfall, was a haven for wildlife. The region's fast-moving rivers and streams were so thick with fat salmon that a few weeks of fishing could provide enough fish, smoked or dried, to last a full year.

Tall, fragrant cedar trees were felled to provide wood for their houses and a variety of hand-carved items such as totem poles, boxes, baskets and eating utensils. Cedar logs were carved out to make

The sea otter population off the coast of British Columbia has increased significantly in recent years, thanks to strict conservation policies. The otters were almost wiped out after more than 100 years of overhunting that began in the middle of the 1800s when Europeans arrived to trade.

Descendants of the once great tribes of Native peoples of the Pacific coast celebrate the spirits of their people and share their culture with the descendents of those who, knowingly or not helped to destroy it.

sturdy canoes decorated with carved designs. Cedar bark was pounded into a form of cloth and made into clothing that withstood the dampness of the rain forest better than the skins and leather hides favored by other tribes of Native North Americans.

During the 1800s, the rest of the world discovered this ideal part of the Pacific coast. At first, the visitors encouraged a trade that brought new wealth to the Native people of the region who received copper and iron for the easy-to-obtain pelts of sea otters. Traders and settlers from Spain, England and China brought not only new tools and new foods, but also new conflicts and new diseases. By the end of the century, terrible epidemics had wiped out much of the population of Pacific people and many towns and villages were permanently abandoned—as were the many reefs, once alive with sea otters that were then almost extinct because of the fur trade.

Magnificent cedar totem poles were carved and placed over doorways and in front yards to honor family spirits. Many are still standing.

A double-decker bus reflects the British character of Victoria, British Columbia.

British Columbia's provincial capital, **Victoria** is the center of life on scenic Vancouver Island. Its climate is the most moderate of any Canadian city. And it is very British. English-style double-decker buses are a common sight in Victoria and most of the city looks as if it might have been built in England and then floated to this beautiful Pacific location. Many residents still take time out every day at 4 o'clock for tea in the British tradition. Like Vancouver, Victoria is a popular place for visitors from around the world.

THE NORTH

Most of the region Canadians refer to as the North is located outside the boundaries of the 10 provinces and is under the direct control of the government of Canada. Around the turn of this century, the North was divided into the **Yukon** and **Northwest Territories**. In 1993, the people of the Northwest Territories voted to carve a third territory out of the eastern section of their land. The new territory, called Nunavut ("our land") will be created as part of an agreement between the Canadian government and the Inuit people who live there. The agreement will allow the Inuit much greater control over their own affairs on land settled by their ancestors some 15,000 years ago.

Most of the North has an arctic climate. Its land and waters are frozen almost year-round. Only in the southern reaches does the ground thaw for a month or two during a summer that would feel more like autumn to most Canadians. The North's climate makes farming all but impossible. Except for fish and game, most food is flown in from southern Canada.

Tourists pose in shorts at the Arctic Circle in mid-summer. They would need long pants and heavy coats for a visit in October.

Some 50,000 people live in the sub-Arctic. They live either in the region's two small cities, **Whitehorse** and **Yellowknife,** or in tiny settlements scattered across a region that represents almost half of Canada's total land mass. Some of these settlements are mining towns that will be abandoned as soon as the mineral being mined runs out. Others

The city of Whitehorse, capital of the Yukon.

A black bear strolls along a riverbank in the Yukon.

serve as supply stations for local trappers, die-hard prospectors and adventurous tourists who really want to get away from it all.

THE INUIT

Only the hardiest of Canada's people, the Inuit, make their permanent home in the frozen Arctic. Historians believe the Inuit were the first Canadians and that they wandered over the North Pole from northern Asia about 15,000 years ago. They were **nomads** who moved from place to place fishing or hunting seeking the fish, whales, caribou, seal, or polar bears that were their only source of life.

In addition to food, these animals also provided the raw materials for Inuit clothing and tools. Skin and fur were stitched together with threads of gristle using needles made from small, sharpened animal bones. Larger bones were carefully carved to make sled runners and **harpoons**—spear like weapons with lines attached so that seal, fish, and even whales, once hooked, could be retrieved from freezing waters.

building an IGLOO

According to this series of photos taken from a 1921 book entitled The Friendly Arctic, *construction of an igloo involves seven steps. These must be completed before "the camp is ready for the night."*

COLD FACTS

Like other groups of Native peoples who have lived close to the land for thousands of years, the Inuit have developed a deep understanding of their environment and the habits of the wildlife who share it. For example, not all ice is the same and the Inuit have several different words for each form. Ice that is created when ocean waters freeze is salty but as it evaporates and then refreezes, it loses its salt and can be melted to provide fresh water for people or sled dogs. Some ice is strong enough to support heavy sleds, while other is partially frozen slush covering icy black water that can swallow up those who break through.

Early sunglasses. This Inuit man wears snow goggles carved from driftwood. The narrow slits protect his eyes from the full effect of blinding light reflected off the pure white landscape.

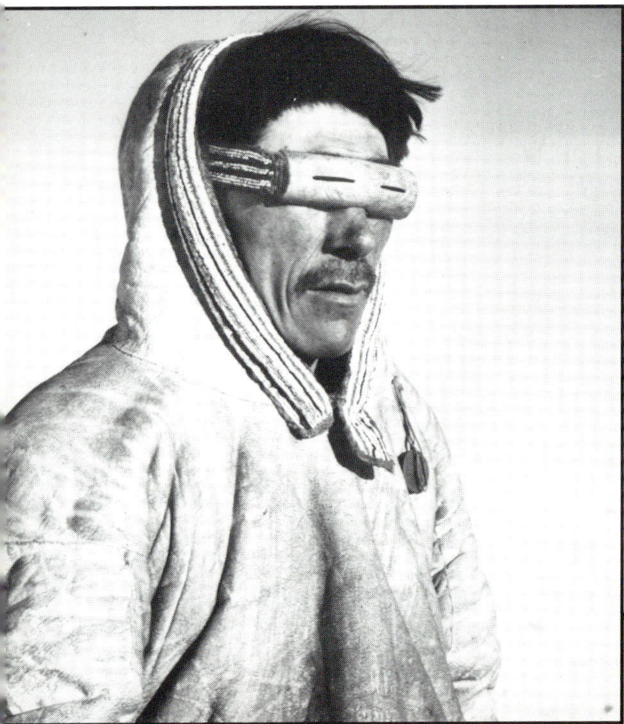

Whatever its form, ice that is not anchored to the land floats on top of salty seas, always in motion because of shifting tides and currents, changing temperatures and, sometimes, heavy winds. As it bends and twists, its moans and groans are often the only sounds breaking the silence of the Arctic.

THE PROBLEMS OF CHANGE

During the last two generations, life for most of Canada's Inuit has been very different from that of their ancestors. During the 1950s, the Canadian government constructed dozens of new villages for the Inuit, complete with schools, hospitals and grocery stores—even television was introduced. The government hoped to make life easier for these long-ignored Canadians whose way of life had changed little for 15,000 years. Its goal was to improve the quality of their lives by offering the Inuit permanent shelter, education and

Inuit art

Inuit carvings and prints are prized by art collectors all over the world. Almost every piece focuses on the Arctic environment. A popular theme is the loving and dependent relationship the Inuit have with their region's wildlife.

Shaman with his helping animals
Ojuitok Ipeelee

better health care. Even those who chose to remain outside of the villages were touched by the modern age. Rifles replaced harpoons, snowmobiles replaced dogsleds, factory-made housing replaced ice-block **igloos.** Started with the best of intentions, the project has had mixed results. Lives have been saved that would have been lost without the medicines and surgery now available in the North. The need to gather food in the wild has, for many, become a thing of the past. Today, cargo planes from southern Canada stock grocery shelves here with a bewildering variety of things to eat. The relocation of the Inuit, however, has also created serious problems.

The Inuit share a love of Arctic wildlife.

The characteristics that make one culture different from another develop out of the life experiences of many generations. Each generation learns the ways of the generations before it and passes them on to the next—like lessons about ice, for example. But lessons learned over thousands of years about

Talking to each other, Irene Tiataalaao

The aurora borealis, or northern lights, can be seen across most of North America, but they are at their brightest and most spectacular where they originate, high above the Arctic ice.

crafting temporary shelters out of ice blocks, hunting and skinning wildlife or managing dog teams, have little meaning or importance to people living in protected villages just down the street from a grocery store.

The first generations of Inuit living in government villages have had a difficult time growing up in an environment where the life lessons of their parents and grandparents do not apply. It has been especially difficult for families living in the smallest and most remote of the villages. Some of the children of these families spend 10 months a year attending large regional schools hundreds of miles from home. Educated by books and television from southern Canada, these children live in a totally different world than their elders, even when they return to share the same house.

A team of huskies pulling a sled designed for the Arctic environment takes a brief rest in the Yukon. The dogsleds are still widely used by hunters and fishers in northern Canada, and racing the sleds is a popular sport in some places. But increasing numbers of people are voicing their objections to the racing, arguing that it is a cruel and inhumane way to treat the dogs.

Like his ancestors, a hunter skins a captured seal in northern Quebec. Many Inuit continue to hunt seals for food and for fur, which they use to make clothing.

A drill bit crunches its way through the Arctic ice and into the ocean floor as its operators search for oil and gas. New technologies have made the once impossible task of drilling for oil in the Arctic not only possible, but also profitable.

COLLIDING ARCTIC WORLDS

Within earshot of Inuit hunters sharpening an animal bone for the day's hunt, powerful high-speed drills with high-tech bits chew through ice and freezing water on their way to tap another pool of oil. A strange new world has arrived on the Arctic landscape.

It is a world of chugging oil rigs and indoor villages that have been carted in by huge ice breakers and aircraft from 3,000 miles away. New advances in resource discovery, well drilling, life support and transportation have made it possible for Canada to realize its dream of being able to tap into the wealth that has been hidden for centuries beneath the Arctic ice. Often separated from their families for weeks at a time, mine workers, oil riggers and engineers have begun to crack open Canada's frozen treasure chest in search of oil, natural gas and other valuable minerals, including a recently discovered source of diamonds.

They live protected from the Arctic's bitter elements in facilities that look like moon dwellings from a science-fiction movie. Here, after work, they can munch on fresh strawberries flown in on daily flights from southern Canada, watch giant video

Whole villages have been designed and constructed in just a few years' time to provide homes for oil workers in the Arctic. Many leave their families behind for months to live and work in the Arctic oil fields.

screens fed by television signals from distant satellites and swim in warm Olympic-size pools. Outside, the Arctic snow swirls unnoticed, carried on howling winds that add an extra bite to temperatures that can drop to -50° F.

So, the land first encountered by its earliest human visitors is today Canada's final frontier. It may turn out to be the site of Canada's most challenging wall of all. Because this is a wall greater than mere distance or language or stone. It is a barrier of many centuries of time, waiting in the North as the keepers of Canada's oldest culture come face-to-face with its newest pioneers. ■

Faster and more reliable air transportation is gradually bringing more exploration and development to the Arctic than ever before. As a result, two very different culture groups once again find themselves face-to-face in North America. Perhaps the lessons learned from past encounters will allow these groups to proceed with greater understanding and fewer disasters.

Questions

1. Why is Vancouver's location on the Pacific Rim important to the rest of Canada?

2. Describe 4 economic activities that are important to the people of British Columbia.

3. What new technologies have allowed Canada finally to begin developing its mineral wealth in the Arctic?

4. How did the relocation of the Inuit affect their culture?

5. WHAT DO YOU THINK? Was the relocation of the Inuit a good idea? Explain.

UNIT 4

MAKING A COUNTRY WORK

THE CHALLENGES OF TODAY AND TOMORROW

Governments are organized so that they may help people work together to solve their problems, to improve their lives, to defend their country and to preserve their environment for future generations.

Canada's great size and the tremendous diversity of its population make governing a very special challenge. However, it is a challenge that must be met as Canada charts its course towards the complex world of the 21st century.

As threats to the global environment grow, as energy sources run low and as old jobs disappear, Canadians know that the regional and ethnic feuding that has occupied so much of their time and energy for so many years is a luxury they will no longer be able to afford.

ESSAY

Life without Canada?

It is one of the saddest facts of life that people seldom realize how much something means to them until it is gone. It applies to almost everything from pet kittens to summer flowers to hot water to childhood to good friends.

What if Canada and everything it has given the world were suddenly to disappear?

There would be no Toronto Blue Jays for Detroit Tigers fans to hate and no Montreal Canadiens for Boston Bruins fans to boo.

There would be a different Captain Kirk at the helm of the starship *Enterprise*, the actor who played the role, William Shatner, was born in Montreal. No *Wayne's World*—comedian Mike Myers is from Toronto—and no *Saturday Night Live*, the show was started by a comedy troup from Ontario. There would be no cold Canadian air for weather forecasters to talk about, and no snowmobiles, basketball, chocolate bars, banana splits or ginger ale—all Canadian inventions.

More serious would be the loss of 29 million Canadian customers who buy millions of dollars worth of American-made products every month. Prices would rise on a wide range of products that Americans now buy from Canada such as lumber, plywood, paper and minerals.

There would be a lot less maple syrup around, and fewer lobsters, salmon and Christmas trees. All of these would be more expensive, too. People planning vacations also would be affected. They would miss out on some of the most beautiful scenery and most exciting cities in the world—including Quebec City with its unique old-world flavor.

Life would be a lot different if Canada suddenly disappeared. . . . *or was no longer our friend.* ■

Christmastime on Parliament Hill. The clock reads five minutes past five o'clock in the afternoon, and it is already pitch black in Ottawa.

CHAPTER 11

Government Decision Makers

TO GUIDE YOUR READING
Look for answers to these questions

1 How did Canada, once a collection of British colonies, become an independent country?

2 Why did Canadians decide on a federal system of government for their country?

3 How does a political party in Canada gain control of the government?

4 What are the responsibilities of the Prime Minister, the Cabinet and the Governor General?

INTRODUCTION

Unlike the United States, which went to war against Great Britain to win its independence, Canada gained its independence through a series of small, peaceful steps that were taken over a period of 200 years following the American Revolution.

*Today, both countries are independent **democracies**. Canadians, like Americans, elect the people who make their laws and lead their government. However, Canada's government is organized differently from the government of the United States.*

CANADA'S CONSTITUTION

Canada became a country on July 1, 1867 when the government of Great Britain approved the British North America (BNA) Act. The act brought together three of Great Britain's North American colonies to create a new country named the Dominion of Canada. The idea came from a group of Canadian leaders, now known as the **Fathers of Confederation**.

The BNA Act also served as Canada's first constitution. The law gave Canadians greater control over their own affairs, but did not make Canada completely independent from Great Britain. The new country remained part of the British Commonwealth and continued to fly the British flag. A representative of the British king or queen, known as the **Governor General**, was given an important role in the government of Canada. The country could not make any change to its constitution without having it approved by Great Britain. Even so, relations between Canada and Great Britain were always friendly and, during the 20th century, Canada gained more and more control over its own affairs. By 1965, Canadians had their own flag.

During the early 1980s, all of Canada's provinces, with the exception of Quebec, reached agreement on changes to the British North America Act that would make Canada completely independent from

Prime Minister Pierre Trudeau and Queen Elizabeth sign the Constitution Act on April 17, 1982. A chilly spring rain could not dampen the enthusiasm of the participants or of the many people who came to watch the ceremony that made Canada a completely independent country.

To the Queen's Most Excellent Majesty:

Most Gracious Sovereign:

We, Your Majesty's loyal subjects, the House of Commons of Canada in Parliament assembled, respectfully approach Your Majesty, requesting that you may graciously be pleased to cause to be laid before the Parliament of the United Kingdom a measure containing the recitals and clauses hereinafter set forth:

A Sa Très Excellente Majesté la Reine,

Très Gracieuse Souveraine:

Nous, membres de la Chambre des communes du Canada réunis en Parlement, fidèles sujets de Votre Majesté, demandons respectueusement à Votre Très Gracieuse Majesté de bien vouloir faire déposer devant le Parlement du Royaume-Uni un projet de loi ainsi conçu:

Annexe A — Schedule A

An Act to give effect to a request by the Senate and House of Commons of Canada

Whereas Canada has requested and consented to the enactment of an Act of the Parliament of the United Kingdom to give effect to the provisions hereinafter set forth and the Senate and the House of

Loi donnant suite à une demande du Sénat et de la Chambre des communes du Canada

Sa Très Excellente Majesté la Reine, considérant:

qu'à la demande et avec le consentement du Canada, le Parlement du Royaume-Uni est

Canada's formal request, in both official languages, to the Parliament of Great Britain for complete control of its constitution, 1981.

Great Britain. The **Constitution Act, 1982** was signed on April 17 by the governments of both Canada and Great Britain. The act gave Canada complete control of its own constitution. A **Charter of Rights and Freedoms** was added so that all Canadians would be guaranteed their rights under the constitution.

A FEDERAL SYSTEM

Because Canada's many regions, and the people who live in them, are so different from one other, governing this country is no easy task. Trying to satisfy the desires of its many different regions and groups is Canada's greatest challenge. Laws acceptable to one part of the country, or one group of people, may cause problems for another.

The issue of language is a good example. Laws passed to guarantee that French Canadians can receive government services in French wherever they travel or live in their country create problems for people living in western Canada where very few people speak French. And the job of printing government booklets, forms and signs in two languages instead of one takes twice as much time, paper and money.

The existence of many regional and cultural differences is one reason why Canada, like the United States, adopted a **federal system** of government. Government powers and responsibilities are shared between the national government and governments of the individual provinces. Provinces have control over their own schools, property laws, health services and natural resources. The government of each province may even regulate trade with other provinces in order to protect its industries from outside competition.

The national government is responsible for military defense, foreign affairs, trade with other nations, money and banking, criminal laws, the mail and most taxes. Canada's national capital is Ottawa, Ontario.

THE CANADIAN PARLIAMENT

Like most democracies in the world, Canada has a **parliamentary** form of government. The job of a parliament is to make the laws and also to put them into effect. The Canadian Parliament consists of the **House of Commons** and the **Senate**.

Canada's Parliament Buildings display the distinctive Gothic style of architecture, as do the British Parliament Buildings in London, England. The style features heavy stone construction with tall, cathedral-like windows, green copper roofing, and many towers, turrets and gargoyles. The building with the clock is called the Peace Tower. It is dedicated to those who fought for Canada in World War I. This view of the Center Block, as it is called, is from the Peace Bridge. The parliamentary library is inside the elaborate cone-shaped structure in the center of the picture.

Members of the House of Commons are elected by the people they represent. Senators are appointed and can serve until they are 75 years of age. They review laws proposed by the House of Commons and often recommend improvements to the way a law is written. But, the House of Commons makes most of the final decisions in Parliament.

Canada is divided into 295 electoral districts called **ridings**. Each is drawn so that it contains about 65,000 people. The people of each riding elect one representative to the House of Commons. They refer to their representative as an MP, the abbreviation for Member of Parliament.

Canada has several **political parties**. Each party has its own ideas about what is good for the country. Each selects a leader to act as spokesperson for the party's views. At election time, the goal of each party is to win the greatest possible number of seats in the House of Commons, because the party with the most seats takes charge of the government. The leader of the winning party automatically becomes Canada's **Prime Minister**. The Prime Minister appoints about two dozen members of the party to be in the **Cabinet.**

The House of Commons. This photo was taken while Brian Mulroney was Prime Minister. He is seen standing at his desk on the left side of the aisle with the other members of his party. The members sitting closest to the Prime Minister are the members of his cabinet. Members who belong to the parties that do not run the government, because they have won fewer seats than the ruling party, sit at desks on the other side of the aisle.

health care in Canada

EVERY CANADIAN HAS ONE OF THESE CARDS. Through their taxes, Canadians support a health-care program that provides them with health insurance. People in need of medical attention visit their doctors or go to hospitals and show this card. The patient never sees a bill. It is paid for by the government—meaning by all the taxpayers of Canada.

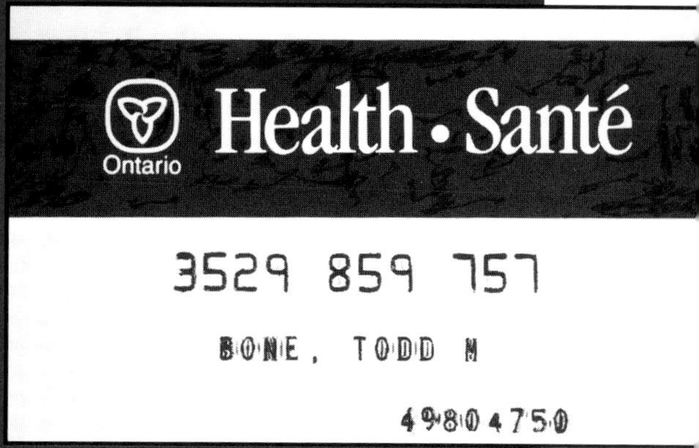

One of the advantages of such a system is that all people can afford medical care, regardless of their income. People who might otherwise put off a visit to a doctor because of the cost are able to seek treatment when they need it. An early visit to a doctor can often prevent a medical problem from becoming more serious, and more expensive, down the road.

Still, the program is not without its problems. Some healthy people who watch their diet, exercise and avoid tobacco and alcohol, resent having to pay for the medical expenses of people who choose to live unhealthy or risky lives. Also, because Canadians think of their medical care as being free, there is great demand for care—some of it unnecessary—which can sometimes cause long waits to see a doctor. According to public opinion polls, however, more than 90 percent of all Canadians are happy with their health-care system.

Each Cabinet member is responsible for a different government department, such as defense, transportation, immigration, or environmental protection. Cabinet members work closely with the Prime Minister to design new laws and programs for the country. Because their party controls the most seats in the House of Commons, their proposals almost always become law.

Once a law has been passed by Parliament, the Prime Minister and the Cabinet must see that it is put into effect by the people who work for the government. These workers form the **civil service**, millions of postal workers, border-crossing guards, law-enforcement agents, forest rangers, tax collectors and many others.

Pierre Trudeau was one of Canada's most colorful, controversial and important Prime Ministers (April 20, 1968-June 4, 1979 and March 3, 1980-June 30, 1984). His government passed the Official Languages Act in 1969, which made Canada officially bilingual. Mr. Trudeau, after many Prime Ministers had failed, managed to broker a deal with the provincial premiers on important changes to the Canadian constitution (up to then an 1867 act of the British Parliament) that created the Constitution Act, 1982. The act made Canada a completely independent nation. Under his leadership, the government of Canada created a new crown corporation named Petro-Canada to take control of the country's oil resources.

Brian Mulroney was Prime Minister (September 17, 1984-May 25, 1993) during one of the most trying decades in Canadian history. It was a decade of tremendous change. Two separate attempts to rework the Canadian constitution in order to bring harmony to the country's divided regions and groups failed. The discussions themselves, designed to heal, seemed only to deepen wounds. Changes in the world economy brought high unemployment to Canada. And a new generation of Native peoples, increasingly aware of, and angry at, the unfairness of their situation, began to press hard for better treatment. Progress was made, but there were some ugly confrontations along the way.

Mr. Mulroney took it in stride. He became a close friend of American President Ronald Reagan and worked to improve Canada's relations with the United States. Together, the two leaders worked out historic agreements between their countries on both trade and acid rain. Mr. Mulroney ignored public-opinion polls that said he was the least popular Prime Minister in 50 years of polling and claimed that he did what he felt was right for Canada's future even if his actions were unpopular when they were taken. Only time will tell if he was right.

Most recent Prime Ministers

Kim Campbell In early 1993, after 10 years in office, and facing another election campaign, Prime Minister Brian Mulroney decided he had had enough of public life. He resigned both as leader of the Progressive Conservative party and as Prime Minister so that the party could select someone new to lead it in the fall election. The party turned to Kim Campbell, a member of the House of Commons from British Columbia and, at that time, Canada's Minister of Defense. As leader of the party, Ms. Campbell automatically became the new Prime Minister, the first woman ever to hold that position in Canada. She was actually quite popular during her few months in office (May 25-October 25), but her party had made too many enemies during the previous 10 years. In the October election, the Progressive Conservatives suffered the worst political defeat in Canadian history. All but two of their members in the House of Commons, including Ms. Campbell, lost their seats.

Jean Chrétien Capping a long career as one of the country's most distinguished and experienced public servants, Mr. Chrétien was named leader of the Liberal Party in 1993. He became Canada's Prime Minister when his party easily won the October, 1993 election. A native of Quebec, he had served in the Cabinet of Prime Minister Pierre Trudeau during the 1970s. He inherited a House of Commons unlike any in Canadian history. One of the two major parties in Canada, the Progressive Conservatives, held only two of the 295 seats in the House, and Mr. Chrétien's Liberals held 178. More than 100 seats were controlled by two new regional parties, one of them devoted to breaking up Canada by promoting independence for Quebec.

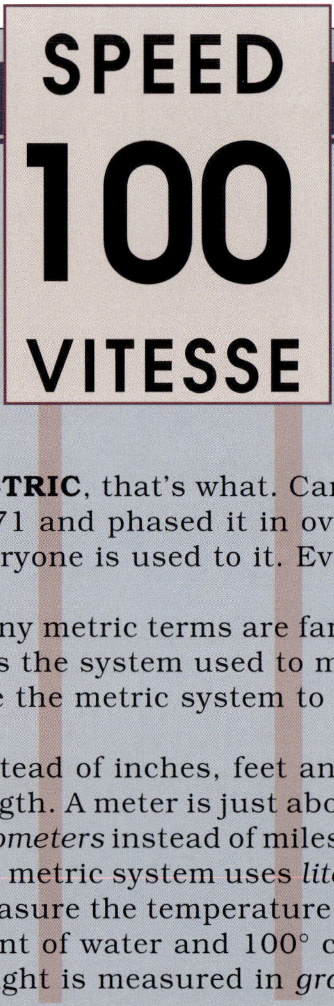

LIVING IN A METRIC WORLD

The speed limit on the crowded highway is 100!

The temperature outside is 25 degrees—and it's the middle of July!

WHAT'S GOING ON HERE?

METRIC, that's what. Canada adopted the metric system of weights and measures in 1971 and phased it in over the following few years. It was difficult at first, but now everyone is used to it. Everyone, that is, except for American tourists.

Many metric terms are familiar to people who follow the Summer or Winter Olympics. It is the system used to measure distances in all events. Most countries in the world use the metric system to weigh and measure.

Instead of inches, feet and yards, Canadians use *millimeters* and *meters* to measure length. A meter is just about 3 inches longer than a yard. For distance, Canadians use *kilometers* instead of miles. A kilometer is 6/10 of a mile. Instead of quarts and gallons, the metric system uses *liters*. A liter is a bit more than the American quart. Canadians measure the temperature of the air in *celsius*. Zero degrees (0°) celsius is the freezing point of water and 100° celsius is the boiling point. Instead of ounces and pounds, weight is measured in *grams* and *kilograms*.

Visitors to Canada should know

- when the speed limit is 100 kilometers per hour, keep it around 60 mph.
- when you're 500 kilometers from Moose Jaw, Saskatchewan, you're closer than you think. It's only about 300 miles down the road.
- When the radio reports that 8 centimeters of snow fell overnight, reach for a pair of boots unless you're wearing high-tops; the snow will be too deep for a pair of dressy shoes.
- for Thanksgiving dinner, a 5-kilogram turkey is about right for 4 people. You've got an 11 pound bird.
- when the temperature is 30° celsius, it's hotter than you think—nearly 90° Fahrenheit. It's a good time to open a liter of cold fruit juice—which will be enough for 4 family members to enjoy about a cup each.

This short poem from Canada will give you a feeling for what celsius temperatures feel like.

0° is cold
10° is not
20° is warm
30° is hot!

Canada has a system of courts to make sure that laws are enforced fairly. Canadian citizens may bring a case to the **Supreme Court** of Canada if they feel that any law interferes with a right guaranteed in the constitution. Justices of the court are appointed by the Prime Minister.

TIES THAT NO LONGER BIND

Canada has maintained its connection to Great Britain and the two countries have a long history of good relations. Canadians have always asked the king or queen of Great Britain to serve as the king or queen of Canada, too.

The monarch is still represented in Canada by the Governor General, who today has only ceremonial duties. He or she welcomes foreign leaders on their visits to Canada and presides over special events such as the **Canada Day** celebration held each July 1st on Parliament Hill in Ottawa. Also, the Governor General still opens each new session of Parliament during a day filled with many traditional ceremonies. They serve to remind Canadians of an earlier time when representative government was not taken for granted, as it sometimes is today. ■

During one of her rare visits to Canada, Queen Elizabeth delivers a speech from the throne in the bright-red, ornate Senate chamber.

Questions

1. Why was the British North America Act important to Canada?

2. What is a federal system of government?

3. How does someone become the Prime Minister of Canada?

4. What does the Parliament do?

5. WHAT DO YOU THINK? Explain at least three features that make the government of Canada *different* from the government of the United States.

THE PICTURES OF THE CANADIAN WOMEN on these pages, from a filmstrip made during the 1950s, hint at what life was like for most married women in North America until the 1960s. The terms *homemaker* and *housewife* were used to describe the majority of women in that era who, once married, were expected to spend their time at home, taking care of young children, preparing meals, sewing, washing and ironing and keeping the house clean and orderly.

Husbands and fathers were expected to hold full-time jobs to support their wives and children. Before the 1960s, when women began to demand a greater role outside the home, most jobs and businesses were dominated by men—except for the brief periods during both world wars when large numbers of women went to work in factories to help the war effort. Some women, most of them unmarried and without children, worked as airline stewardesses, secretaries, nurses, maids, teachers, librarians or entertainers, and that was about all. Women doctors, lawyers, business executives, politicians, television announcers, carpenters or plumbers were extremely rare. Though more women have now entered all of these fields, in each one they are

still greatly outnumbered by men. And, on average, men earn more money for the same work.

The business of government was also traditionally considered to be men's work. Both the American and Canadian constitutions were written by groups of men—the Founding Fathers and the Fathers of Confederation. No mothers were invited to participate. The government of Canada denied women the right to vote for their member of Parliament until 1918. Most provinces waited even longer than that to allow women the right to vote in provincial elections. Quebec waited until1940.

Canada's 1982 Charter of Rights and Freedoms prohibits discrimination based on sex. Such a guarantee has yet to be added to the Constitution of the United States. By 1993, Canada had its first woman Prime Minister and many women had been elected to the House of Commons and appointed to the Cabinet and Senate. Today, more than half of all Canadian women, many of them wives and mothers, hold jobs outside the home.

THE MOVE TOWARD EQUALITY

a new role for women in modern Canada

CHAPTER 12

Facing the Future

A major challenge facing both Canada and the United States is finding a new approach to living in harmony with their Native peoples.

TO GUIDE YOUR READING
Look for answers to these questions

1. What difficult choices face Canadians as they develop their natural resources?
2. What challenges face Canada as it seeks to protect the rights of its various ethnic minorities and language groups?
3. Why is Canada's friendship important to the United States?
4. What is Canada's role in the world community?

INTRODUCTION

During most of the 20th century, Canada has made its living sawing, mining, drilling, fishing and then selling its natural resources to the rest of the world. All the while, the country has been distracted by almost constant quarreling among its various regions and its two founding peoples, the French and the English. Even so, during this century, Canada built a successful manufacturing base and came of age as an important trading partner and ally of the United States as well as a valuable member of the world community.

As they prepare for life in the next century, Canadians are taking a hard look at their future. Many know that resource development cannot continue as it has if Canada is to protect its natural environment and that regional squabbling cannot be allowed to persist if Canada is to remain united.

Decisions Canada makes during this decade will affect its future relations with the United States and with the rest of the world during the 21st century.

RESOURCE DEVELOPMENT AND THE ENVIRONMENT

Regardless of how much land or how many resources a country has, no country has enough to waste, not even one as large as Canada. As Canada has developed into a modern industrial nation, its citizens have maintained a strong love of the outdoors and respect for the natural environment. Both are deeply rooted in the beliefs and traditions of the Native peoples who had a powerful influence on the country's earliest explorers and settlers.

Living in a country whose national identity has always been closely tied to its wilderness, Canadians remain committed to protecting as much of their soil, natural vegetation, water resources and wildlife as they can. But because Canada's most valuable resources are located in the forests, under the ground and beneath the sea, it is impossible to develop them without disturbing

Acid rain is formed when smoke from factories in the industrial heartlands of Canada and the United States rises high into the atmosphere and drifts over the eastern parts of both countries. There it may be washed out of the sky and carried to earth by rain or snow.

the natural environment. The challenge is to use it without destroying it.

Nature depends on new growth to repair damage done to plants and animals. In the North, where so much of Canada's mineral wealth remains untapped, natural growth is extremely slow. It takes a very long time to repair any damage caused by even the most careful development. Accidents resulting in fires or spilled oil or chemicals can be disastrous. It is possible to cause damage that can never be repaired.

Pipeline construction, while necessary for a growing economy, detracts from the natural beauty of the wilderness. Also, above-ground pipelines can interfere with the migratory patterns of the wildlife that roams the North in search of food. Bridges are built at various places along the pipelines to allow wildlife to cross.

One result of resource development is the **pollution** of lakes and streams. Water pollution is not only ugly, but dangerous as well. Pollution makes water unsafe for drinking or for irrigation and gardening. It also makes water poisonous to fish and then to the birds and shore animals that eat them. Even recreation is affected. Water pollution in some of the Great Lakes became so bad by the 1980s, for example, that it threatened to ruin freshwater fishing in the region.

ACID RAIN

Scientists believe that the pollutants carried to earth by acid rain are responsible for damage to lakes, rivers, streams, forests and wildlife in eastern Canada and the United States.

The air, too, has become polluted in many parts of North America and the effects are just as serious. The abundance of coal in the United States and Canada makes it a popular fuel in both countries. Millions of tons are burned each year to generate the electricity that powers machinery in large manufacturing plants. Smoke from many coal and oil burning plants in the industrial midwestern United States and in southeastern Canada is washed out of the sky by the snow and rain that falls east of the Great Lakes. The pollution, called **acid rain,** may be responsible for damaging millions of square miles of forest land, small lakes and topsoil in both countries.

The leaders of Canada and the United States continue to search for a solution to the problem of acid rain, but it is not an easy one to solve. Cleaning smoke before it is released into the air or changing to new fuels are expensive measures. When required to take such measures, manufacturers are often forced to raise the prices of the products they make and sell. Some have moved out of North America to set up plants in countries that have fewer restrictions. That puts people out of work.

If acid rain continues to fall, however, entire forests may be destroyed and thousands of lakes may lose their fish and other forms of life.

A hydroelectric complex at James Bay, showing the enormous reservoir behind the dam as well as the powerhouse and spillway. Developing any form of energy resource presents difficult choices for people who also want to protect the natural environment.

ELECTRICITY FROM JAMES BAY

One solution to the problem of acid rain is to find another energy source that is as inexpensive as coal, but cleaner. During the early 1970s, the government of Quebec believed it had the answer. It began construction of a huge hydroelectric project on the eastern edge of James Bay in the northern part of the province. The **James Bay Project**, being built in several phases, already holds back the waters of many large rivers flowing into James Bay with a series of huge dams made of sand, gravel and glacial material. Water at the dams is released in controlled, yet forceful, streams to turn giant electric turbines. The turbines generate clean electricity which lights homes and powers factories in eastern Canada and the northeastern United States.

By the time construction on Phase 1 was completed, it was clear that the project had environmental problems of its own. The damming of the rivers would flood huge areas that for thousands of years had been home and hunting ground for the region's Native people, the **Cree**. These areas had also been grazing land for the caribou and the habitat of many other species of wildlife important to the Cree livelihood.

A debate over whether to go ahead with additional construction in the region currently rages across Canada and in the American states that were planning to purchase power from the site. The question is simple, though the answer is not: Is having the capacity to generate more electricity worth the flooding of hundreds of square miles of Canada's natural environment, or should people who use electricity learn to use less?

Hydro-Québec workers replant trees on piles of earth removed during the construction of dams near James Bay. Some 11 million bushes and trees—mainly fast-growing green alder, jack pine and willow—have been planted throughout the construction site.

THE SEARCH FOR OIL

Another difficult choice is whether to go after any more of the oil that is known to exist beneath the ocean floor off Newfoundland, Nova Scotia and New Brunswick. It is risky business. The cold, rough waters of the north Atlantic are peppered with icebergs, some as big as shopping malls, that have broken off the Arctic ice pack 2,000 miles to the north. The icebergs are a constant threat to the floating oil rigs needed to get at the oil, and also

Floating rigs like this one in the north Atlantic off the coast of Newfoundland provide a platform for oil-drilling equipment built to tap pools of oil and natural gas beneath the ocean floor. Icebergs and heavy seas are a constant threat in the offshore-drilling business.

to the enormous tankers that transport it to land. A broken pipe or ruptured tanker could send millions of gallons of sticky black goo floating across the water, suffocating fish and poisoning vegetation and wildlife when it washes up on shore.

But the risk is tempting because the oil lies off the coasts of Canada's poorest provinces where at times nearly one out of every five people cannot find a job. Development of the nearby oil resources could produce thousands of jobs in the region and provide badly needed income for these provinces and for the rest of Canada, as well.

CONFLICTS OVER LANGUAGE AND CULTURE

Canada is trying to bring to an end the quarreling among its different regions and its two founding peoples. However polite the quarrels have been, they have taken up a lot of time and energy. Studies and opinion polls show that the vast majority of Canadians now want to redirect their efforts towards preparing their country for the 21st century. But that is easier said than done.

Most countries have a hard enough time trying to manage their affairs in one language. Canadians conduct theirs in two. The country is officially **bilingual**. Its bilingualism policy is deeply rooted in Canadian history. When England defeated France in 1763 and took control of North America, it guaranteed the French people living there that they could maintain their language and culture. Throughout its history, Canada has struggled to protect the spirit of that policy.

According to the **Official Languages Act, 1969**, all services, activities, signs and printed materials prepared by the Canadian government must be available in both French and English. The more recent Charter of Rights and Freedoms affects the provincial governments, as well. It guarantees that English Canadian and French Canadian citizens have the right to receive government services in their own language in every part of the country.

The charter, however, is part of the new Canadian Constitution. And when it went into effect in 1982, Quebec refused to sign it. Its government felt that the constitution did not allow the province enough power to protect its French language and culture.

Surrounded by members of his cabinet, Prime Minister Pierre Trudeau receives an ovation from the House of Commons after announcing the agreement that led to the Constitution Act, 1982.

Since then, Quebec has been trying to convince the rest of Canada to grant it special powers over its own affairs. At the same time, many people in Quebec have argued that their province should declare its independence and become a separate country. Most of these people, called **separatists**, believe that an independent Quebec could remain friendly with the rest of Canada and with the United States. In 1980, when asked to vote on the question of separation, the citizens of Quebec voted to remain part of Canada.

René Lévesque, the founder of the Parti Québécois. This political party's goal is to separate Quebec from the rest of Canada in order to form a separate country. The party won control of the Quebec government in the 1976 provincial election and did so again in 1994.

If such a vote were held today, however, the outcome might be different. In 1987, Prime Minister Brian Mulroney brought the provincial **premiers** together to work out an agreement that would allow Quebec finally to sign the constitution. Their meeting was a success. The Prime Minister and the premiers called their agreement the **Meech Lake Accord**. However, in order for it to go into effect, the accord had to be approved by the governments of all the provinces within three years. When the deadline arrived in 1990, Quebec was disappointed. The governments of both Manitoba and Newfoundland decided not to support the agreement. Many French Canadians in Quebec were angry and began to talk of separation once again. Others joined the rest of Canada in still another search for the right plan to keep their country together.

As Quebec has increased its demands for more power to protect French Canadian culture in the province, Canada's Native peoples have also begun to push for constitutional guarantees that would help protect their way of life. They are especially annoyed by the Official Languages Act, 1969 that recognizes the French and the English as Canada's two founding peoples. They feel the law ignores their existence as the true founding peoples of Canada. In 1991, the Canadian government proposed a plan that would gradually allow Native peoples in Canada greater control over their own affairs within 10 years It is not clear, however, whether it will go into effect because many Canadians oppose the plan.

Bilingual signs in Montreal are scarce these days because of a recent law that strictly limits the use of languages other than French on most outdoor signs in the province of Quebec.

Ovide Mercredi, leader of the Assembly of First Nations, played an important and vocal role in organizing Canada's Native peoples and negotiating with the Canadian government during the early 1990s.

The Official Languages Act, 1969 left its mark on packaging in Canada.

EAST VERSUS WEST

Quebec is not the only place where there has been talk of separation. Some people in western Canada have claimed that they, too, should form a separate country. Many of their leaders have complained that the government of Canada has gone too far in trying to satisfy the people of Quebec.

Canada's Ambassador to the United States explained it this way in 1991: "People in western Canada are saying, if the people in Quebec want more power because they are different, what about us?"

The question has special meaning in the 1990s because, for the first time in the country's history, the population of western Canada is now larger than the population of Quebec.

Separated from eastern Canada by the rock and forest of the Canadian Shield, western Canadians have long felt left out of their country's important affairs. For years, they were distant bystanders as government officials in Ottawa debated issues dealing with English and French relations in eastern Canada. The topic was of little interest in the west where few French Canadians live. But western Canada became suddenly very interested when the government of Canada passed the Official Languages Act.

Soon, the French language was visible in western Canada wherever government business was done. Post offices in western Alberta got new signs that read "Postes Canada Post" even if no one within a hundred miles spoke French. Because the law requires bilingual packaging on products sold across Canada, western Canadians found strange new words appearing on everything they bought in their stores: *Les chien chauds* was printed on packages of hotdogs, *lâit* and *crème* on cartons of milk and cream. Some western Canadians were angry and frustrated.

All government services in Canada must be offered in the languages of both official founding peoples, the French and the English—even in western Canada where there are only a very few French-speaking Canadians.

Today, with more people and greater wealth, western Canada has put the rest of the country on notice that it expects a greater share of power in the national government.

RELATIONS WITH THE UNITED STATES

Like any relationship between close friends, the Canada-United States relationship has had its ups and downs. Coloring every part of it is the huge difference in population size. Although the two countries are similar in physical size, the population of the United States is 10 times greater than the population of Canada. About 80 percent of Canadians live within 100 miles of the Canada-United States border.

Speaking to an American audience, one of Canada's former Prime Ministers, Pierre Trudeau, explained why Canadians are sensitive about having such a powerful neighbor: "Living next to the United States is in some ways like sleeping with an elephant. No matter how even-tempered is the beast, one is affected by every twitch and grunt."

Someone else has said, "When the United States sneezes, Canada catches cold."

The two countries are each other's most important trade partners, so when the American economy hits bad times, Canadians know that they are in for trouble, as well. Because Canada and the United States are allies, when the threat of war hangs over the United States, it also—like acid rain—hangs over Canada. And because Canada and the United States share the Great Lakes and many rivers, when one country pollutes the water, both countries suffer the consequences.

Because almost every Canadian can receive at least one American television channel and only a few Americans are able to watch television from Canada, Canadians tend to know a lot more about the United States than most Americans know about Canada. That is beginning to change, however, as technology and trade tie the fortunes of the two countries even closer together. As Americans learn how important Canada is to their future, they will want to learn more about Canada and the people who call it home.

The election of Brian Mulroney as Prime Minister in 1984 was a turning point in the Canada-United States relationship. He quickly became a close friend of American President Ronald Reagan. Together, the two leaders convinced their governments to pass important new laws promoting trade and reducing acid rain.

A SPECIAL WORLD ROLE

Measured by military might, Canada is far from being a world power. Still, over the last 50 years, Canada has played an important role in helping to shape world events. The fact that Canada is a country of several languages and cultures may give its leaders and diplomats special insight into the problems that divide people in other countries. Even if their record has not been perfect, Canadians are greatly respected in the world community because of their long history of trying hard to accept and protect cultural differences in their own country.

As an active member of the **United Nations** and the **League of Nations** before it, Canada has been asked on many occasions to help settle arguments between nations and even to go to war. Canada has been a willing supplier of aid for the victims of wars and natural disasters, and has stationed its troops as peace-keepers in a number of countries. Today, the world is watching Canada, hoping that it will be able to solve its own problems in the 1990s. If it can, Canada may provide a model that could help change the world for the better during the 21st century. ■

Questions

1. Name two forms of pollution and tell how each one affects the environment.
2. Why was the Official Languages Act, 1969 resented by some people in western Canada?
3. Why did Quebec refuse to sign the Constitution Act, 1982?
4. How is Canada affected by its location next to the United States, a country with 10 times as many people as Canada?
5. WHAT DO YOU THINK? What difficult choices are involved in trying to deal with the problem of acid rain?

Canadian soldiers wearing the uniform of the United Nations. Canada has a long-standing reputation for fairness and thoughtful independence in the world community of nations. As a result, it has been asked on many occasions to help solve disputes between quarreling nations or to act as a peacekeeper in war-torn areas.

ACROSS CANADA, thousands of descendants of North America's Native peoples make their homes on large tracts of land separate from the laws and everyday life of the rest of Canada. Several of these tracts of land, called reserves, extend into the United States. Despite the influences of modern technologies, native traditions on the reserves have been kept alive for many thousands of years.

Still, many of these reserves are today islands of hopelessness and despair. Native people living on the reserves have seen progress and development pass them by, partly as a result of their own choices—choices rooted in their traditions and values. A new generation of Native peoples see the affluence of modern Canada that exists outside the reserves and are angry that it all seems so utterly beyond their reach. Frustrated and confused, many have turned to alcohol and other dangerous drugs—even to suicide—thus putting the future of their own children in jeopardy. And so the cycle continues. It is a tremendous challenge for both Canada and the United States.

Life on the reserves

CANADA'S NATIONAL HOLIDAYS

Abraham Lincoln's birthday passes with little fanfare in Canada, and Canadians aren't any more excited about the fourth of July than they are about the third. Canada has its own special days. Here are a few.

VICTORIA DAY

May 24

or the Monday before

Victoria Day is one of the oldest holidays on the North American Continent. Young Canadian school children remember the day with a rhyme: "It's the 24th of May, the Queen's Birthday, if we don't get a holiday, we'll all run away." The day celebrates the birthdays of both Queen Victoria and Queen Elizabeth II. Queen Victoria was Queen when Canada became a nation in 1867. Queen Elizabeth signed the Act which made Canada completely independent from Great Britain in 1982.

REMEMBRANCE DAY

November 11

Canada has had a strong history of honoring its war dead since the end of World War I. Once celebrated as part of the Canadian Thanksgiving, Remembrance Day has been celebrated on November 11 since 1931. During the week before the holiday, members of the Royal Canadian Legion distribute red poppy flower pins across the country which are worn in a united show of appreciation for Canadians who gave their lives in war.

CANADA DAY

July 1

Canada Day celebrates the country's birthday. It was July 1, 1867 when the British North America Act created a new country called Canada from three British colonies in North America.

Also celebrated as holidays are

Christmas
•
New Year's Day
•
Easter
•
Labor Day
•
Canadian Thanksgiving Day

. . . and holidays from all over the world are celebrated in the many large ethnic communities across Canada.

The only birthdays celebrated as national holidays in Canada are those of Queens Victoria and Elizabeth. No Canadian—not even the country's first Prime Minister—has been honored with a national holiday.

CANADIAN *as a second language*

THE ENGLISH LANGUAGE as spoken by many—but not all—Canadians has its own character, which, in part, reflects Canada's long and close relationship with Great Britain. Canadians still use a number of different expressions for some of the words Americans commonly use. Below, the Canadian words are red and the American words are white.

American	Canadian
athletic shoe	sneaker
pitcher	jug
fifth grade	Grade 5
folks	parents
lollipop	sucker
grades	marks
rubber band	elastic
silverware	flatware
huh?	eh?
closet	cupboard
camp	cottage
swimsuit	bathing suit
vacation	holiday
strainer	seive
alley	lane
deck (of cards)	pack (of cards)

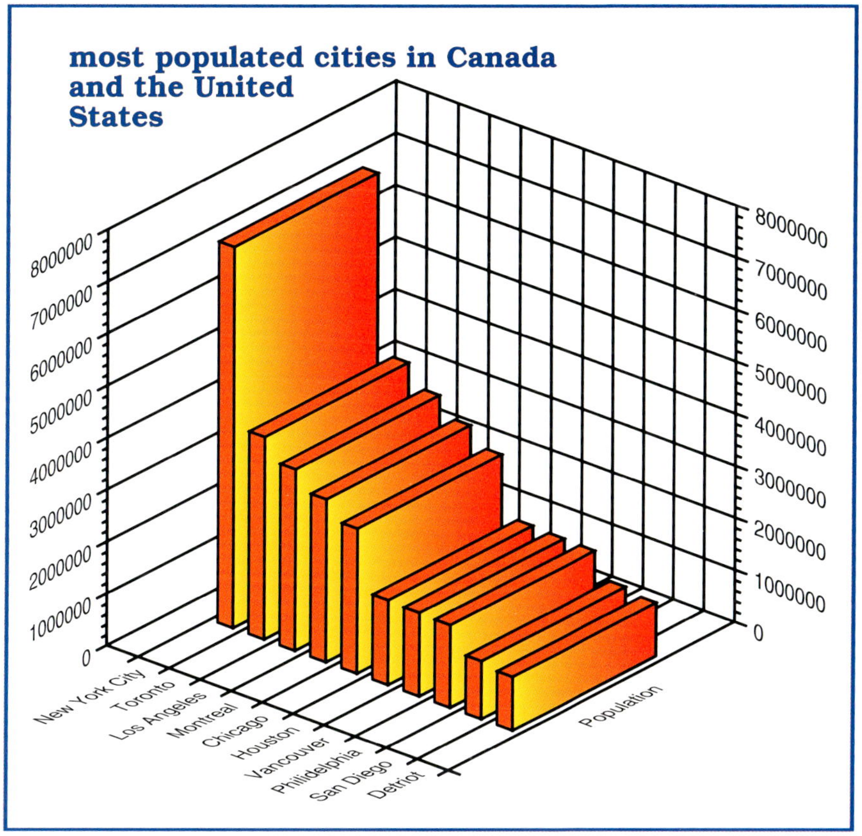

GLOSSARY OF BOLD-FACED TERMS

Terms appear in bold-face type the first time they appear in the text. See index on page 215.

A

Acadia Believed to be the first European colony in North America, Acadia was located on the Bay of Fundy near the Gulf of St. Lawrence in what is today Nova Scotia. France surrendered the colony to England in 1713. The English renamed it Nova Scotia and, in 1755, forced some 8,000 French Acadians to leave their homes for refusing to pledge loyalty to England in its looming war with France.

acid rain Rain that carries smoke pollution back to earth. Most scientists believe that the pollutants found in acid rain are harmful to vegetation and animal life.

Act of Union, 1841 British law that united the colonies of Upper and Lower Canada to create a single colony called the United Canadas.

agriculture Farming; raising food from the land.

Alaska Between 1867 and 1959, before becoming a state, Alaska was a territory. Disagreement over Alaska's southern border caused a serious dispute between the United States and Canada during the late 1800s and the first few years of the 1900s.

Alberta The westernmost of Canada's prairie provinces, Alberta is located between Saskatchewan and British Columbia.

Appalachian Mountain System Mountain system that stretches from Newfoundland and northern Quebec southward along the Atlantic coast to central Georgia in the southeastern United States.

archipelago An area of many closely packed islands.

arctic climate The climate of the North. Winter temperatures can drop to -50°F; summer temperatures seldom rise above 60°F. In the far reaches of the North, the temperature almost never goes above freezing. Snowfall is very light because the bitterly cold air is so dry.

Arnold, Benedict General in the Revolutionary War who joined forces with General Robert Montgomery for an attack on Quebec City in 1775. The attack was a dismal failure. Arnold later changed loyalties and joined the English to fight against independence for the colonies.

Atlantic Canada Term used to describe Canada's four easternmost provinces: Newfoundland, Prince Edward Island, Nova Scotia and New Brunswick.

B

bilingual A bilingual person can comfortably speak two languages. Bilingual signs or brochures are printed in two languages. Canada is officially bilingual: by law, all government documents and services are provided in both French and English.

British Columbia (colony) Established in 1750, the colony joined the Dominion of Canada in 1871 after Canada's first Prime Minister, John A. Macdonald, promised to link it with the provinces of eastern Canada by building a transcontinental railroad.

British Columbia (province) Canada's westernmost province. Important because of its location on the Pacific Rim.

British Commonwealth of Nations Today the commonwealth is a loose, voluntary association made up of Great Britain and most of its former colonies. When Canada was born in 1867, it, along with Newfoundland (which did not join the Canadian Confederation until 1949), joined Australia, New Zealand and South Africa as dominions in the British Commonwealth. As such, these countries had control over most of their internal affairs but remained tied to Great Britain by a mutual defense agreement.

British North America (BNA) Act The 1867 British law, based on a plan presented by a group of Canadian leaders known as the Fathers of Confederation, that created the Dominion of Canada. The new country was initially made up of only four provinces (Quebec, Ontario, Nova Scotia and New Brunswick).

C

Cabinet The group of individuals selected by the Prime Minister to head the various executive departments in the Canadian government, such as finance, foreign affairs and fisheries. Its job is to implement and enforce the laws of Parliament that deal with its area of responsibility and to suggest new laws its members feel are necessary.

Cajun Acadian culture found in southern Louisiana, especially in New Orleans. Some of the Acadians who had been forced from their homes in Nova Scotia by the English in 1755 for refusing to take a loyalty oath to Great Britain wound up in southern Louisiana. At that time Louisiana was still controlled by the French. The blending of their culture with those of other settlers in the region, many of whom were from nearby Caribbean Islands or Spain, resulted in a unique style of cooking featuring spicy dishes that take advantage of local sea foods. The term *Cajun* resulted from a careless pronunciation of *Acadian*.

Calgary The second largest city in the province of Alberta.

Calgary Stampede Annual summer event held in Calgary, Alberta, that draws thousands of participants with a variety of western activities such as rodeos, country-music concerts, barbeques and wagon races.

Canada Day National holiday that marks the signing of the British North America Act (on July 1, 1867) and the creation of the Dominion of Canada. The holiday was called Dominion Day until 1982.

Canadian Pacific Railway Canada's first transcontinental railroad. A major engineering feat, it had to cross the towering Rocky Mountains in order to link the Pacific-coast province of British Columbia with the rest of the country.

Canadian Shield A vast area of solid rock that sprawls across east-central Canada and into the North, and that covers about one-third of the Canadian land mass. Though heavily forested in some of its southern reaches, it is mostly covered with marshes, lakes, exposed rock and, in the North, ice and snow. Most of its mineral wealth is yet to be tapped.

caribou Large, reindeerlike animals which inhabit the Canadian North. They travel in herds and are important to the culture and livelihood of the Inuit and other Native peoples of the region.

Cartier, Jacques Believed to be the first French explorer of North America. He made three trips up the St. Lawrence River during the mid-1500s, searching for gold and a water route to China. Disappointed over Cartier's lack of success, the king of France ended his support for any further North American adventures until Samuel de Champlain was commissioned in 1604 to establish a French presence in North America and to cultivate the fur trade.

Champlain, Samuel de Known as the father of New

France, Champlain spent the better part of his adult life exploring, mapping and trying to encourage French settlement in North America. But, because the king of France offered little support to the early French colonies in North America, during Champlain's lifetime New France was little more than a far-flung network of small farms and forts with a tiny population of wandering traders and priests.

Charlottetown Prince Edward Island's capital, largest city and only important port. It was at Charlottetown that Canada's Fathers of Confederation first met in the early 1860s to discuss the idea of Canadian Confederation.

Charter of Rights and Freedoms Canada's Bill of Rights. The individual rights of Canadians have been protected in writing for a half century, but they were guaranteed in statute, not in a constitution. When Canada gained complete control over its own constitution in 1982, a new Charter of Rights and Freedoms became part of the Constitution Act.

civil service The collectivity of government workers, including postal workers, customs agents, inspectors, and so on.

Civil War Often referred to as the War Between the States. Feeling threatened by the election of Abraham Lincoln to the presidency in 1860, 11 southern states that depended on enslaved people for labor, broke from the United States hoping to form a separate country. Lincoln's attempt to preserve the union resulted in a long and bloody conflict between North and South. The war ended in victory for the North. Many Canadians joined the northern cause to fight against slavery.

CN Tower Located on the Toronto waterfront, this telecommunications tower, owned by the Canadian National Railway, is the tallest freestanding structure in the world. Visitors can eat in a revolving doughnut-shaped restaurant, and the very brave can be whisked by elevator up to an observation deck near the top to be treated to a breathtaking panoramic view of more than 100 miles on a clear day.

Coureurs de Bois The term means "runners of the woods." Most were very young men who, instead of establishing a farm and family, lived by their wits—hunting, fishing and trading with the Native peoples, or doing odd jobs in the towns and villages sprouting up along the St. Lawrence River.

Confederate States of America The collection of southern states that separated from the United States over the issue of states' rights and slavery in 1861, following the inauguration of Abraham Lincoln. They were forced back into the union after a long civil war.

confederation A country made up of individual states or provinces that retain a good deal of authority over their own affairs. The United States was a confederation until 1789. Canada is a confederation to this day.

Constitution Act, 1791 British law that divided the Quebec colony into Upper and Lower Canada. The law was designed to accommodate the large number of loyalists who had already settled in the western part of the colony, far from the original French-speaking inhabitants of the St. Lawrence Valley.

Constitution Act, 1982 Agreed to by both Canada and Great Britain, this law amended the British North America Act, 1867 to create a completely independent Canada and a new Canadian constitution that included the Charter of Rights and Freedoms.

continental climate A climate that features hot summers and cold winters with fairly even precipitation throughout the year. There are no distinct wet or dry seasons. Far from the moderating influences of the ocean, much of the interior of North America has a continental climate.

cultural mosaic A collection of many national and ethnic groups living within the same country. Instead of being encouraged or forced to conform to a single culture, groups are encouraged to maintain and celebrate their differences while living in harmony with a common citizenship. Canada's official policy of multiculturalism is designed to foster such an ideal.

Cree The Native people of central Quebec who live near James Bay. The traditional way of life of the Cree is threatened by hydroelectric development along rivers flowing into James Bay.

crown corporations Government-owned businesses in Canada such as the Canadian Broadcasting Corporation (CBC), Petro-Canada and the Canadian National Railway (CNR).

D

democracies Countries that have a form of government in which the people have the power to manage their own affairs, usually by electing representatives to make and enforce their laws.

diversity When applied to the study of people, this term refers to groups that embrace a variety of languages and cultures, usually the result of considerable immigration. Both Canada and the United States are countries with cultural diversity. When applied to geography, the term refers to areas of many and varied landforms, such as ocean coasts, mountain systems, plains and plateaus.

Dominion of Canada The name given to the new country formed in 1867 when Great Britain passed the British North America Act. The British government, at the urging of both English- and French-Canadian leaders, divided the huge United Canadas colony into the provinces of Quebec and Ontario and joined them with Nova Scotia and New Brunswick to form the Dominion of Canada.

E

Edmonton Capital of, and largest city in, Alberta.

F

factory farms (or mechanized farms) Huge farms on which most of the work is done by machinery requiring only a few farmworkers. Most are owned by large food companies that mass produce a few specialized products for grocery stores, fast-food chains and restaurants across Canada and the United States. Products include potatoes, corn, soybeans and beef. It is becoming more and more difficult for small farmers to compete with these factory farms.

Fathers of Confederation Canada's founding fathers. The group of French- and English-Canadian leaders who negotiated and designed the Canadian Confederation. Their ideas formed the framework for the British North America Act, 1867, which established the Dominion of Canada.

federal system A system of governing a country in which powers are divided between the national government and the individual states or provinces.

founding peoples The first people to inhabit an area. According to Canadian law (the Official Languages Act, 1969), Canada recognizes two founding peoples, the French and the English. The law guarantees access to federal government services in the languages of both peoples. However, it also annoys many of Canada's Native peoples, whose ancestors were the country's original inhabitants. They feel it ignores their status as the real founding peoples of Canada.

Fraser Delta Fertile agricultural region in southern British Columbia at the mouth of the Fraser River. The region has a climate moderate enough to support a prosperous, if small, fruit and vegetable industry.

Fraser River Long, meandering river in British Columbia that originates in the Rocky Mountains. The river runs north, then bends to flow southward and empty into the Pacific Ocean in the southwestern corner of the province near Vancouver.

Fredericton City located in the center of New Brunswick on the Saint John River. Though considerably smaller than the port city of Saint John, Fredericton is the political, cultural and educational capital of the province.

French and Indian War Also known as the Seven Years War; the final struggle between England and France for control of North America. The French surrendered soon after losing a major battle fought on the Plains of Abraham in Quebec City in 1759. The English forces were led by General James Wolfe, the French forces by General Louis-Joseph de Montcalm. Both generals lost their lives on the battlefield.

G

Governor General The monarchy has always been, and still is, the ceremonial head of the Parliament of Canada. The Governor General represents the monarch when he or she is not in Canada, and opens each new session of Parliament and performs various other largely ceremonial duties.

Grand Banks Huge, flat, underwater plateau off Canada's Atlantic coast. Its shallow waters provide an ideal environment for fish to breed and grow. Huge pools of oil and natural gas have been discovered beneath the ocean floor in the Grand Banks.

H

habitants Peasant farmers of New France. The word means "settlers" in French

Halifax (city) Nova Scotia's capital, and its largest city and port.

Halifax (port) Located on the east coast of Nova Scotia, this bustling port is free of ice all year long. Established by the English in 1749, it has long been one of the largest naval bases in North America.

harpoons Long spearlike weapons with attached lines. The hunter or fisher tosses the harpoon at creatures in the water, such as seal or whale, and retrieves the captured prey by pulling in the line.

Hibernia Oil Field Area where large pools of oil and gas were recently discovered, but are still untapped, off the southeast coast of Newfoundland beneath the Grand Banks. Unemployed workers in Atlantic Canada would benefit from jobs created by its development, but oil companies are not sure if they would be able to earn back what would be a costly investment. People concerned about the environment oppose developing this oil field because of the great numbers of icebergs in the area that could cause tremendous damage if they were to hit a drilling platform or tanker.

House of Commons Body of 295 elected members that represents the people of Canada. Each member holds a seat, and represents a designated legislative district, called a riding. Legislative activities of the House are controlled by the political party that holds the majority of seats (either alone or in cooperation with another party).

Hudson's Bay Company British trade company, formed in 1670, that controlled the fur trade in the vast territory between the Great Lakes and Hudson Bay and the Northwest Territories for more than 200 years.

Hull A city on the Ontario-Quebec border located on the Ottawa River directly across from Ottawa. Together, the two cities form Canada's National Capital Region. They are linked by several bridges, including the Peace Bridge, a symbolic joining of Canada's two founding peoples.

Huron Native people who inhabited the lands in the St. Lawrence River Valley in what is today southern Quebec.

Hydroelectric Production The generation of electricity by huge turbines that are turned by fast-flowing water at dams built across large rivers.

I

igloos Dome-shaped dwellings crafted from blocks of ice or snow. Traditional shelter of the Inuit people of the North.

immigration Moving to, and taking up residence in, a country after leaving one's homeland.

Inuit Native people of the North.

Iroquois Native people who lived in what today is the Adirondack Region of northern New York State. The Iroquois were successful farmers and trappers—and fierce warriors. In the struggle for control of the North American fur trade, the Iroquois were allied with the British while their historic rivals, the Huron, were allied with the French.

J

James Bay Project One of the largest hydroelectric development areas in the world. A series of dams built on rivers that flow into the eastern side of James Bay.

Joliet, Louis Joliet and Catholic priest Father Jacques Marquette were the first French explorers to travel the Mississippi River. Together they sailed half of its length in 1673.

L

Labrador Name given to the half of the province of Newfoundland that is located on the Canadian mainland.

***la conquete* (the conquest)** The term used by French Canadians to describe the defeat of French forces in North America. The decisive battle was fought on the Plains of Abraham in Quebec City in 1759. The English forces were led by General James Wolfe, the French forces by General Louis-Joseph de Montcalm. Both generals lost their lives during the battle.

lake-effect snow Snow formed when warm, moist air passes over unfrozen lakes and collides with cold air over land. It is most common along the eastern shores of the Great Lakes in both Canada and the United States, usually in the very late autumn.

Lake Ontario One of the five Great Lakes shared by Canada and the United States.

La Salle (René-Robert Cavelier, Sieur de La Salle) Nine years after the voyage of Joliet and Marquette, La Salle claimed the Mississippi River and much of the surrounding land for France. He named the area Louisiana, after Louis XIV, king of France.

latitude Measures distance from the equator in units called degrees. Latitude is shown by parallel lines on a map.

Laurier, Sir Wilfred The first French-Canadian Prime Minister; Laurier was in office from 1896 to 1911.

League of Nations First World organization dedicated to maintaining peace and encouraging democratic ideals through cooperative and collective action. The brainchild of American president Woodrow Wilson and part of the famous 14-point Versailles Treaty that ended World War I, the league was generally ineffective and was dissolved following Japan's unchecked invasion of the Chinese province of Manchuria in 1933. The United States Congress refused to approve the treaty, and the country never joined the league. Canada, however, was an active and supportive member from the beginning.

Lincoln, Abraham Sixteenth president of the United States, who served from 1861-1865. His inaugural pledge to forbid the expansion of slavery to any territory where it did not already exist led to the secession of 11 southern states and touched off the Civil War.

Louisiana Claimed and named for France by René-Robert Cavelier, Sieur de La Salle in 1682, the Louisiana territory was a huge area of land fronting the Gulf of Mexico and extending inland several hundred miles on both sides of the Mississippi River. After the French were defeated in the last of the so-called French and Indian Wars, the territory west of the Mississippi was given to Spain as part of the Treaty of Paris, 1763. Spain later gave it back to the French. In 1803, President Thomas Jefferson negotiated the sweetest land deal since the sale of Manhattan. For 15 million dollars, Jefferson purchased for the United States the vast territory west of the Mississippi to the Rockies and north to Canada, doubling the size of the country. Its appetite whetted, the expansionist young nation was fighting in Canada nine years later for even more territory.

Lower Canada One of the two colonies created by the Constitution Act, 1791, a law passed by the Parliament of England. To accommodate the large number of loyalists who had settled in the western part of the Quebec colony during and after the American Revolution, the British government divided Quebec into Upper and Lower Canada. The area where most of the loyalists had settled, north and west of lakes Erie and Ontario, became Upper Canada. Lower Canada was situated along the St. Lawrence River Valley, where most of the original French settlers in Quebec had made their homes.

loyalists Americans who refused to join the war for independence against England, preferring to remain loyal to the king. Many were publicly humiliated and physically harmed as a result. Thousands fled the United States, both during and after the Revolution and headed for the British colonies that would later become Canada. Their arrival eventually led to the creation of two new Canadian colonies, Upper Canada (which later became the province of Ontario) and New Brunswick, which was carved from land in western Nova Scotia.

M

manufacturing Creating products from natural resources.

Macdonald, John A. First Prime Minister of Canada. He was instrumental in establishing Canada as an independent and prosperous country. One of his most important accomplishments was the successful completion of Canada's first transcontinental railway.

Manitoba Easternmost of the prairie provinces, located between Ontario and Saskatchewan.

Manitoba Act, 1870 Act of the Canadian Parliament that created the province of Manitoba. The act was passed only after serious negotiation and compromise with the Native inhabitants of the area, the Métis, who opposed any westward expansion into their territory. The government promised the Métis that their French language and culture would be protected.

Maritimes Refers collectively to the closely-tied Atlantic provinces of Prince Edward Island, Nova Scotia and New Brunswick.

maritime climate A climate experienced by coastal regions. Maritime weather is characterized by abundant rainfall and temperatures that are moderated by ocean waters. Except in the extreme north, the moisture and moderate temperatures combine to support the growth of lush vegetation and thick forests.

Marquette, Father Jacques (see Joliet, Louis)

mechanized farms (see factory farms)

Meech Lake Accord In 1987, Prime Minister Brian Mulroney brought the 10 Canadian provincial premiers together to work out an agreement that would allow Quebec finally to sign the Canadian Constitution Act, 1982. The result of their meeting was the Meech Lake Accord. In order to go into effect, the accord had to be approved by the governments of all the provinces within three years. When the deadline arrived in 1990, both Manitoba and Newfoundland refused to support the agreement.

melting pot A society formed by blending together many cultures, each one contributing a unique aspect to the national culture that all members are expected to embrace.

Métis Descendents of the early French fur traders who married into the Native population. The Métis developed a unique culture that reflected their French and Native heritage. Several hundred Métis were living in what is today southeastern Manitoba when, during the late 1860s, agents of the Canadian government arrived to pave the way for new settlement. Fearing for the future of their French language, Roman Catholic religion and land, the Métis decided to resist any attempt to bring new people to the West. (see also Riel, Louis)

Montgomery, Richard General in the Revolutionary War who joined forces with General Benedict Arnold for an attack on Quebec City in the fall and winter of 1775. The attack failed, and Montgomery lost his life in the battle.

Montreal Located on an island in the St. Lawrence River, Montreal is the largest city in the province of Quebec and the largest French-speaking city in North America.

Mount Royal Mountain landmark in the heart of Montreal. A favorite spot for city residents and tourists alike because of its wooded parks, sleigh and carriage rides and captivating views of the surrounding city.

multiculturalism Official policy adopted by Canada to foster the ideal of many national and ethnic groups living in harmony in the same country. Instead of conforming to a single culture, Canadians are encouraged to maintain and celebrate their differences while sharing a common citizenship.

Murray, James The popular and pragmatic governor of the Quebec colony immediately following the Conquest whose suggestions and concerns led to the passage of the Quebec Act, 1774. Its generous provisions allowed the French Canadians living in the colony the right to maintain their own language and culture.

musk ox Large, shaggy, horned mammal, native to the Canadian Arctic and Greenland.

N

National Policy Prime Minister John A. Macdonald's three-point program for the development of Canada, which he announced in 1878. It was a plan to encourage the growth of industry in the East, to increase immigration to the West and to provide money for the transcontinental railroad he promised the new province of British Columbia.

natural regions Areas of the earth's surface defined by their geography. Canada has six distinct natural regions.

natural resources Products of nature such as fertile soil, fresh water, wood and minerals.

Native peoples Term used to describe the original inhabitants of North America. They arrived from Asia more than 15,000 years before the settlers came from Europe.

New Brunswick One of Canada's Atlantic provinces. It has the second-largest population of French Canadians after Quebec.

New Brunswick (colony) Many American United Empire loyalists escaped to the Nova Scotia colony and settled in the fertile Saint John River Valley and along the northern shore of the Bay of Fundy. A community of 14,000 eventually managed to build a thriving colony far removed from Nova Scotia's original settlers and their government. In 1784, the region was marked off from the rest of the Nova Scotia peninsula as the separate colony of New Brunswick.

Newfoundland The most remote of the four provinces in Atlantic Canada. Only half of the province, called Labrador, is part of the Canadian mainland. The other half, where most of the people live, is an island about the size of Tennessee. Newfoundland remained a British colony until 1949, when its people voted in a referendum to become the 10th province of Canada.

nomads People who have no permanent residence and wander from location to location in search of food.

North Region that covers the top half of the Canadian land mass. The region has an arctic climate and is treeless, though in some places a short summer thaw supports the growth of a surprising variety of small, colorful forms of vegetation.

NORAD (North American Aerospace Defense Command) A cooperative effort between Canada and the United States after World War II resulted in the integration of the air defense forces of both countries under a single command, NORAD, at Boulder, Colorado. It was formed to guard the skies over North America and repel a possible air attack from the former Soviet Union.

Northwest Mounted Police Police unit formed to pave the way for an orderly and nonviolent expansion and settlement of western Canada during the late 1800s. The name was later changed to the Royal Canadian Mounted Police (RCMP), and is often shortened to the Mounties.

Northwest Rebellion The second of two rebellions by the Native Métis against westward expansion led by Louis Riel. It took place in what is today southern Alberta and Saskatchewan, and was quickly put down by the Northwest Mounted Police. Riel was captured and hanged for treason.

Northwest Territories (NWT) Actually, only one territory. During the late 1800s, the Canadian government created two territories, the NWT and the Yukon, from its holdings in the North. The land had previously been controlled by the Hudson's Bay Company and named Rupert's Land. The NWT is located north of Manitoba, Saskatchewan and Alberta. (see also Nunavut)

Nova Scotia One of Canada's Atlantic provinces.

Nova Scotia (colony) After losing one of its many wars with England, France surrendered Acadia in 1713. England changed the name of its new colony to Nova Scotia.

Nunavut In 1993, the people of the Northwest Territories voted to create a third territory in the North. Called Nunavut, or "our land," the new territory is the result of an agreement between the Inuit people who live there and the Canadian government. The agreement will allow the Inuit greater control over their own affairs on land settled by their ancestors 15,000 years ago. The territory is to be fully operational by the end of this century.

O

Official Languages Act, 1969 According to this law, Canada must be officially bilingual. The law requires all federal government documents and services to be provided in both French and English.

Ontario Canada's second-largest province in size, its largest in population, and the heartland of English Canada.

Ohio River Valley Triangle-shaped, fertile valley south of the Great Lakes between the Ohio and Mississippi rivers. Rich with beaver, the valley was the scene of considerable fighting between the French and English and their Native allies during the days of the fur trade. The valley was also attractive to prospective settlers. They were angered when the English government declared the region off-limits in the Royal Proclamation, 1763 and then made it part of the Quebec colony in 1774.

Ottawa Canada's capital; located in eastern Ontario on the Ottawa River across from Hull, Quebec. Together, the two cities form Canada's National Capital Region. They are linked by several bridges, including the Peace Bridge, a symbolic joining together of Canada's two founding peoples.

P

Pacific Rim Land surrounded by or bordering the Pacific Ocean. It is an area of rapid economic development and increasing international trade.

parliamentary (form of government) In this type of government, the majority party (the party that holds the greatest number of seats in the House of Commons) rules. The ruling party controls lawmaking in the House and also carries out the laws by taking charge of the civil service.

permafrost A condition of the land found in the Canadian North. The ground there is permanently frozen except for a brief period during the summer, when a few inches of topsoil may thaw and support some fast-growing vegetation. Permafrost makes development, including rail or highway construction, very difficult.

petro-chemical industry Industry associated with various products that are derived from petroleum (oil).

plain A landform, near sea level, that is flat. Plains are usually fertile because most were once a part of the ocean floor that has recently been raised above sea level.

plateau A landform located high above the surrounding terrain. Unlike a mountain, a plateau is quite flat.

polar bear White bear of the Arctic.

polar ice caps Northernmost reaches of the Arctic surrounding the North Pole where the ice and snow never melts.

political parties Organizations of individuals who share similar ideas about what is good for their country. Political parties try to gain control of the government by winning elections so they will be able to put their ideas into effect.

pollution chemicals and other types of airborne and waterborne particles, some of which may be harmful to vegetation, wildlife and humans.

Pontiac, Chief Native American chief who, in 1763, led a group of Native tribes to capture most of the English forts west of Niagara. England, having just won control of the area after the so-called French and Indian War, realized that the desires of the Native people would have to be taken into account. In the Royal Proclamation, 1763, King George III declared the land west of the Appalachians off-limits to English settlement.

Port Royal The first permanent French settlement in North America. Located on the Bay of Fundy in what is today Nova Scotia, the settlement was established by Samuel de Champlain in 1605.

Prairie Region A fertile plain that extends from the western edge of the Canadian Shield to the base of the Rockies.

premier The leader of a province in Canada. Each of Canada's 10 provinces has a parliamentary form of government.

Prime Minister The leader of the political party that holds the greatest number of seats in the House of Commons becomes Canada's Prime Minister. While serving as an elected member of the House of Commons, the Prime Minister also is in charge of the government bureaucracy and speaks for Canada in its dealings with foreign countries.

Prince Edward Island The smallest of Canada's provinces, this scenic island in the Gulf of St. Lawrence is a popular summer vacation spot for Canadians and Americans because of its tranquil, rural way of life and many miles of beautiful, sandy beaches.

Q

Quebec Act, 1774 This Act of the Parliament of England, passed 15 years after the Conquest (see conquete, la), guaranteed French Canadians living in Quebec the right to maintain their own language and culture. The law's generous provisions had a practical side. The English hoped to gain the loyalty of the people of Quebec to prevent them from joining the independence movement brewing in the original 13 colonies to the south. The act also enlarged the boundaries of the Quebec colony to include the fertile land between the Ohio and Mississippi rivers.

Quebec City Capital city of the province of Quebec. The original fortress, located high on a cliff overlooking the St. Lawrence River, was Canada's first true city, and the site of the decisive battle in 1759 that ended French rule in North America.

Quebec (colony) Until 1763, the boundaries of the Quebec colony were fuzzy. The colony roughly encompassed the St. Lawrence River Valley from the Gulf of St. Lawrence southwest to the Ottawa River Valley. It was given more clearly defined boundaries by the provisions of the Quebec Act, 1774. The act greatly enlarged the size of the Quebec colony by including the fertile land of the Ohio River Valley within its borders.

Quebec (province) Canada's largest province in size, second in population, and the heartland of French-Canadian language and culture.

R

regional diversity Geographers use this term to describe countries, like Canada, that contain many different natural regions within their borders.

reserves Across Canada, thousands of descendents of North American Native peoples make their homes on large tracts of land, called reserves, that are separate from the laws and culture of the rest of the country. Several of the reserves extend into the United States, a reminder of the days before European settlers divided the land with man-made boundaries. Despite the influence of modern technologies, Native traditions on the reserves have been kept alive. Still, many of the reserves are islands of hopelessness and despair. Many young Native people look at the affluence that surrounds them off the reserves and are angry that it all seems utterly beyond their grasp. Frustrated and confused, a number of them have turned to alcohol and other dangerous drugs—even to suicide—thus endangering the future of their own children. And so the cycle continues. The problem represents a tremendous challenge both for Canada and the United States.

ridings Canadian legislative districts. Each riding is represented by one member of the House of Commons.

Riel, Louis After leading the Métis people in two rebellions against Canadian westward expansion, Riel was arrested and tried for treason. Despite pleas from the Roman Catholic church and French Canadians across the country, Riel was found guilty and put to death by hanging. His story is one of most controversial in Canadian history. Although he was found guilty of being a traitor to Canada, his bravery on behalf of the Métis made him a hero to French-speaking Canadians, who were feeling increasingly threatened by the rapid expansion of English Canada.

Rocky Mountains The imposing, scenic mountains

that stretch north and south along the western coast of Canada.

Royal Proclamation of 1763 After Chief Pontiac captured a series of British forts in the Ohio Valley, King George III declared the land west of the Appalachians off-limits to English settlement. The act angered the English colonists. It was one of the first of many more serious rifts between the colonies and the Crown that eventually led to the American Revolution.

rural Country areas away from cities and towns. Rural areas are sparsely populated and include villages and family farms.

S

Saint John Largest city and most important port in New Brunswick.

St. Lawrence River The most direct inland route to the heart of North America from Europe. The river originates in the northeast corner of Lake Ontario and flows northeastward to empty into the Gulf of St. Lawrence and the Atlantic Ocean.

St. Lawrence Seaway A series of canals and locks along the upper St. Lawrence River to allow the passage of heavy ocean-going vessels to and from the Atlantic Ocean and the Great Lakes. Until the Seaway was built, dangerous rapids and shallow water between Montreal and Lake Ontario prevented large boats from traveling on the upper part of the river. Building the seaway was a cooperative project of the United States and Canada that began in 1950. It opened in 1959.

St. Lawrence River Valley The flat, fertile valley that borders the St. Lawrence River between Montreal and Quebec City. The valley was the heartland of New France and home for most of its first permanent settlers, or *habitants.*

Saddledome The city of Calgary's huge enclosed stadium where indoor rodeos are held and where Calgary's hockey team, the Flames, play home games.

Saskatchewan One of Canada's prairie provinces, located between Manitoba and Alberta.

Senate One of two houses of the Canadian Parliament. Its members are appointed by the Prime Minister when a vacancy occurs (either through resignation or mandatory retirement at age 75). The Senate has the power to veto laws passed by the House of Commons, but it has not done so since 1940. It has played a useful role in suggesting amendments to legislation under consideration by the House of Commons, and has conducted numerous investigations into a variety of important and often controversial topics. The Senate has 104 members; 24 each from Quebec, Ontario and the four western provinces; 30 from the Atlantic provinces; and one each from the Yukon and the Northwest Territories.

separatists People in Quebec or in western Canada who support the idea that their region should break away from the rest of Canada to form a separate, independent country.

Seven Year's War (see French and Indian War)

Sherbrooke A small city in southeastern Quebec originally settled by United Empire Loyalists from New England and northern New York State.

SkyDome The futuristic enclosed stadium—with a retractable roof—that is the home of the Toronto Blue Jays baseball team as well as the Toronto Argonauts of the Canadian Football League.

St. John's Newfoundland's capital, largest city and port.

sub-Arctic The southern portion of the Arctic where, during the summer months, some of the land thaws for a short while and comes alive with a variety of lush vegetation and colorful wildflowers.

Supreme Court Canada's highest court. The Constitution Act, 1982 and the Charter of Rights and Freedoms have broadened the role of the court to include judicial review and the definition of rights listed in the charter. There are nine members of the Supreme Court: three from Quebec, three from Ontario, two from western Canada and one from the Atlantic provinces.

T

tar sands Much of the oil in western Canada is found near the surface, soaked into the soil, instead of being found in liquid pools between the layers of rock that make up the earth's crust. The oil in these tar sands can be extracted, but the process is slow and expensive.

Tecumseh, Chief In defending their homeland during the War of 1812, Canadians received valuable help from Chief Tecumseh and his band of Native warriors, who joined the battle on the side of the English hoping to block further westward expansion by the United States.

terrain This term means "the lay of the land, and refers to visible landforms such as mountains, rocks, plains and plateaus.

topography (see terrain)

Toronto Located on the western shore of Lake Ontario, Toronto is Canada's largest city and the capital of the province of Ontario. It is also the country's financial capital and the media and cultural capital of English Canada.

trade The exchange of goods and services between countries and states, provinces and people.

Treaty of Paris, 1763 The treaty signed following the defeat of France by England in the Seven Year's War. France surrendered all of its claims to land in North America except for two tiny islands in the Gulf of St. Lawrence. The Louisiana territory west of the Mississippi went to Spain for its help in the war against France. The treaty gave England control over a North American empire that stretched from the Atlantic Ocean to the Mississippi River and from Hudson Bay to the Gulf of Mexico.

Trudeau, Pierre One of Canada's most colorful, controversial and important Prime Ministers (serving from April 1968 until June 1979, and March 1980 until June 1984). His first government passed the Official Languages Act, 1969, which made Canada officially bilingual. Trudeau, though many Prime Ministers had failed to do so before, managed to broker a deal with the provincial premiers on important changes to the Canadian constitution (up to then, an 1867 act of the British Parliament) that created the Constitution Act, 1982. The act made Canada a completely independent nation.

tundra The treeless region in Canada's North. Because of the cold and dry climate, only a few natural grasses, mosses and lichens are able to grow there during the short summer months.

turbines Made to spin at high speeds, usually by water power, these machines create electricity. Sixty percent of Canada's electricity is generated by turbines in a process called hydroelectric production. Much of Canada's hydroelectric power travels through thousands of miles of thick steel cables to be sold in the United States.

U

Underground Railroad For several decades before the Civil War, as many as 50,000 enslaved people from the southern United States escaped from their owners and fled to Canada, where slavery had already been outlawed. A network of home owners in the northern states provided food and shelter for them along the way. Each stop was referred to as a station, and the network became known as the Underground Railroad.

United Canadas The colony created by the Act of Union, 1841. The United Canadas colony combined the former colonies of Upper and Lower Canada.

United Nations (UN) Organized in 1945 immediately following World War II, the United Nations is a world organization made up of more than 180 countries whose goal is to avoid conflict between peoples and nations and, through cooperation, to search for ways to bring an end to hunger, disease, poverty and violations of human rights. Canada has traditionally been one of the UN's most active and supportive members.

Upper Canada One of two colonies created by the Constitution Act, 1791 to accommodate the loyalists who had settled in the western part of the Quebec colony during and after the American Revolution. The British government divided Quebec into Upper and Lower Canada. Upper Canada was where most of the loyalists had settled, north and west of lakes Erie and Ontario.

urban Anything related to cities. An urban environment usually features densely populated residential areas made up of apartment houses, hotels and condominiums, with crowded streets, office buildings and shopping complexes. Also present are restaurants, theaters, cultural centers and professional-sports facilities.

V

Vancouver The largest city in British Columbia and one of Canada's fastest-growing and most important centers. Although the city has long been isolated by its remote location (on the Pacific Coast facing Vancouver Island), improvements in transportation and communication have made this spectacularly beautiful place more accessible to the rest of Canada and to the rest of the world—especially to the rapidly growing nations of the Pacific Rim.

Vancouver Island Large, scenic island located off the southern coast of British Columbia. Its Pacific location provides Vancouver Island with the most moderate climate found in Canada.

Victoria Capital city of British Columbia, located on Vancouver Island.

voyageurs The *voyageurs*—or "travellers," in French—crisscrossed most of North America by canoes (and by foot when they had to), to expand the fur-trade network for France during the 1600s and 1700s.

W

War of 1812 During the early 1800s, renewed warfare between England and France eventually affected American trade and interests. The British practice of hijacking American sailors and forcing them to serve in the English navy infuriated the people of the United States. Expansionists in Congress took advantage of the angry climate to push their case for a land-grab invasion of Canada. Fought with equal fury on land and sea, the war soon ground down to a draw and, in the end, the United States failed to gain any new territory. For Canadians, their success in turning back the American invasion was a source of great pride.

war hawks Members of the United States Congress in the early 1800s who favored going to war against Great Britain both to avenge the English navy's practice of forcing American seamen into service and to gain territory by conquering the British colonies in Canada.

West Edmonton Mall Located in a suburb of Edmonton, Alberta, the West Edmonton Mall is the largest indoor shopping and entertainment complex in the world.

World War I This war began in 1914 and was an important turning point in the Canada-United States relationship. With Great Britain under attack by Germany and its allies, Canada, as a member of the British Commonwealth of Nations, had little choice but to join the war. Nearly 61,000 Canadian soldiers lost their lives during the war, proportionally more than those of any other country. The United States tried to remain neutral, but it could not. With its ships under attack by German submarines and democracy threatened in Great Britain and France, the United States decided to enter the conflict. In 1917, it sent millions of young soldiers, sailors and pilots across the Atlantic to fight. The huge and well-equipped American forces were too much for the enemy to handle. The war ended in 1918, and Canadian and American troops returned home to help build a new relationship between their two countries.

World War II Once again, Canada declared war on Germany and its allies just days after the British did so in 1939. In 1941, the United States joined the war and again fought side by side with Canada to defend democracy in Europe. As was the case during World War I, the cooperative effort of Canada and the United States served to bring the two countries even closer together.

Winnipeg Often referred to as the Gateway to the West, Winnipeg is the capital of, and the largest city in, Manitoba.

Y

Yukon During the late 1800s, the Canadian government created two territories from Rupert's Land, its vast holdings in the North that had previously been controlled by the Hudson's Bay Company. These were named the Yukon and the Northwest Territories. The Yukon is located north of British Columbia.

INDEX

OF BOLD-FACED TERMS

NOTE: Page numbers in *italics* indicate illustrations or their captions. Page numbers for the *Glossary* (pp. 203-214) are followed by *a* for terms found in the left column, and *b* for the right column.

PHOTO CREDITS

Photographs are listed by page, from top to bottom (side-by-side photos are listed L to R). See page ii for a complete listing of the agencies and individuals who supplied photographic images for this text.

(PAC = Public Archives of Canada)

COVER Metropolitan Toronto Convention and Visitors Association; (inset photos) Tourism British Columbia; Francis Anne Hopkins, PAC (c-2771); Travel Manitoba.

BACK COVER Ontario Ministry of Tourism and Recreation; (inset photos, clockwise from top left) Dan Heringa, NWT Economic Development and Tourism; Ottawa Tourism and Convention Authority; Ministère du tourisme du Québec; Toronto Blue Jays; Ministère du tourisme du Québec.

OPENING PAGES
Ministère du tourisme du Québec.
Tourism New Brunswick.
Francis Anne Hopkins, PAC (c-2771).
Travel Manitoba.
Tourism Vancouver.

TABLE OF CONTENTS Government of Saskatchewan Photographic Services Agency; Nova Scotia Tourism; NWT Economic Development and Tourism; Ontario Ministry of Tourism and Recreation; PAC (c-114484); PAC (c-57); PAC (c-14220); PAC (c-14464); Ministère du tourisme du Québec; Travel Manitoba; Katsunori Nagase, NWT Economic Development and Tourism; Ottawa Tourism and Convention Authority; Gulf Canada Resources Limited.

UNIT 1

page 2: Yukon Government Photo.
page 4: Dennis Hulbert.

CHAPTER 1

page 6: Tourism New Brunswick; Tourism New Brunswick.
page 7: John Sylvester, PEI Tourism.
page 8: Nova Scotia Tourism; Nova Scotia Tourism; Barrett and MacKay, PEI Tourism.
page 9: Nova Scotia Tourism.
page 10: Ministère du tourisme du Québec.
page 11: Ministère du tourisme du Québec.
page 12: Inco Limited; National Film Board of Canada.
page 13: Travel Manitoba; Calgary Convention and Visitors Bureau; Yukon Government.
page 14: Tourism British Columbia.
page 15: Calgary Convention and Visitors Bureau.
page 16: NWT Economic Development and Tourism.
page 17: Ed Struzik, NWT Economic Development and Tourism.

CHAPTER 2

page 19: Tourism British Columbia.
page 20: NWT Economic Development and Tourism.
page 21: Wolfgang Webber, NWT Economic Development and Tourism.
page 22: PEI Tourism.
page 23: Travel Manitoba.
page 24: Ministère du tourisme du Québec.
page 25: Ministère du tourisme du Québec; Montreal Visitors and Convention Bureau.
page 26: Ontario Ministry of Tourism and Recreation.

CHAPTER 3

page 28: Tourism British Columbia.
page 29: Barrett and MacKay, PEI Tourism.
page 30: Ottawa Tourism and Convention Authority.
page 31: Tourism New Brunswick.
page 32: Tourism New Brunswick.
page 33: John Sylvester, PEI Tourism; National Film Board of Canada; National Film Board of Canada.
page 34: National Film Board of Canada; Tourism British Columbia;
PAC (pa-11566).
page 35: Inco Limited; Inco Limited.
page 36: Gulf Canada Resources Limited; Bow Valley Energy, Inc.; Petro-Canada; TransCanada Pipelines Limited; Imperial Oil Limited.
page 37: Imperial Oil Limited; Shell Canada; Petro-Canada.
page 40: Hydro-Québec.
page 41: Hydro-Québec.
page 42: Barrett and MacKay, PEI Tourism.
Yukon Government.
page 43: Ministère du tourisme du Québec.

UNIT 2

page 44: Hervey Smyth, PAC (c-788).
page 46: PAC (c-101995).
page 47: John Verelst, PAC (c-92419).

CHAPTER 4

page 48: J.E. Laughlin, PAC (c-120844).
page 49: PAC (c-3278).
page 50: PAC (c-99068).
page 51: Charles William Jefferys, PAC (c-103059).
page 53: PAC (nmc-24731).
page 54: George Agnew Reid, PAC (c-11013).
page 55: Francis Anne Hopkins, PAC (c-5188); Coke Smyth, PAC (c-1026).
page 57: Charles William Jefferys, PAC (c-73448).
page 58: PAC (c-82974).
page 59: PAC (c-16415).
page 60: Robert Hood, PAC (c-40364); Gudin, PAC (c-7182).
page 61: Charles William Jefferys, PAC (c-69559).
page 62: PAC (c-24563); F.D. and Charles Copeland, PAC (c-19584).
page 63: Louis-Joseph Watteau, PAC (c-3704).
page 64: Charles William Jefferys, PAC (c-69728); Charles William Jefferys, PAC (c-73439); James Peachey, PAC (c-2029).
page 65: Allain Manesson Mallet, PAC (c-107626).

CHAPTER 5

page 67: PAC (c-73418).
page 69: Charles William Jefferys, PAC (c-70317), PAC (c-70318).
page 74: Hy. Sandham, PAC (c-168).
page 77: PAC (nmc-126160).

CHAPTER 6

page 78: PAC (pos-2214).
page 80: Lorne K. Smith, PAC (c-11052).
page 81: Charles William Jefferys, PAC (c-70229).
page 82: J.O. Davidson, PAC (c-4847); Major Dennis, PAC (c-276)
page 83: PAC (c-41067).
page 84: Cornelius Krieghoff, PAC (c-11214
page 85: PAC (pa-147950).
page 86: PAC (pa-164728).
page 88: PAC (pa-17369).
page 89: PAC (pa-168973).

CHAPTER 7

page 90: Canadian Embassy.
page 91: PAC (c-26461).
page 92: PAC (pa-800424).
page 93: PAC (c-3693); PAC (mg26, a, vol.129, p. 53567).
page 94: PAC (pa-181359); PAC (pa-38064)
page 95: PAC (c-6688 d); PAC (c-17240).
page 96: PAC (pa-10237); PAC (c-9671).
page 97: PAC (c-52819, c-30621); PAC (pa-38567).
page 98: Canadian Consulate General; Cantwell, photo no. 46, Special Collections Division, University of Washington.
page 99: PAC (c-16459).
page 100: PAC (c-73392); PAC (pa-66544).
page 101: PAC (pa-41785); PAC (pa-10265).
page 102: PAC (c-87550); PAC (pa-568).
page 103: A.R., PAC (c-95728); PAC (c-97750); Mary Riter Hamilton, PAC (c-132006).
page 104: PAC (c-80917); PAC (pa-145952); PAC (pa-803553).
page 105: Nichol, PAC (c-033441); Marian Scott, PAC (c-087493); Leo Bachle, PAC (c-99610).
page 106: National Film Board of Canada.
page 107: C.J. Patterson, PAC (c-111243).
page 108: PAC (pa-103542); PAC (c-46350).
page 109: pa-103543); Max Gamper, PAC (c-105622).

UNIT 3

page 110: Ministère du tourisme du Québec.
page 112: Dan Heringa, NWT Economic Development and Tourism; PAC (pa-10237).
page 113: Metropolitan Toronto Convention and Visitors Association.

CHAPTER 8

page 114: Tourism New Brunswick.
page 115: Wayne Sturge, Government of Newfoundland and Labrador.
page 116: Nova Scotia Tourism; Wayne Sturge, Government of Newfoundland and Labrador.
page 118: Nova Scotia Tourism; Wayne Sturge, Government of Newfoundland and Labrador.
page 119: Barrett and MacKay, PEI Tourism, Barrett and MacKay, PEI Tourism.
page 120: Ministère du tourisme du Québec.
page 121: Ministère du tourisme du Québec; Ministère du tourisme du Québec.
page 122: Ministère du tourisme du Québec; Ministère du tourisme du Québec; Ministère du tourisme du Québec.
page 123: Ministère du tourisme du Québec; Ministère du tourisme du Québec.
page 124: Ministère du tourisme du Québec; Ministère du tourisme du Québec.
page 125: Canadian Government Travel Bureau.
page 126: Ontario Ministry of Tourism and Recreation.
page 127: Metropolitan Toronto Convention and Visitors Association.
page 128: Metropolitan Toronto Convention and Visitors Association; Sid Barren, *Toronto Star*, May 23, 1969, PAC (c-133345); Metropolitan Toronto Convention and Visitors Association.

page 129: Ontario Ministry of Tourism and Recreation.
page 130: Metropolitan Toronto Convention and Visitors Association; Toronto Blue Jays.
page 131: Metropolitan Toronto Convention and Visitors Association; Metropolitan Toronto Convention and Visitors Association.
page 132: Ottawa Tourism and Convention Authority.
page 133: Ontario Ministry of Tourism and Recreation.
page 134: Ottawa Tourism and Convention Authority; Ontario Ministry of Tourism and Recreation.
page 135: Ottawa Tourism and Convention Authority; Inco Limited.

CHAPTER 9

page 136: Government of Saskatchewan Photographic Services Agency.
page 137: Government of Saskatchewan Photographic Services Agency.
page 138: Orest Semchishen.
page 139: Government of Saskatchewan Photographic Services Agency.
page 140: Petroleum Communication Foundation.
page 141: Calgary Convention and Visitors Bureau.
page 142: West Edmonton Mall.
page 143: West Edmonton Mall.
page 144: Calgary Convention and Visitors Bureau.
page 145: Calgary Convention and Visitors Bureau.
page 146: Calgary Convention and Visitors Bureau.

CHAPTER 10

page 148: Tourism British Columbia.
page 149: Tourism British Columbia.
page 152: Tourism British Columbia.
page 153: Tourism Vancouver.
page 154: Tourism Vancouver.
page 155: Tourism Vancouver.
page 156: Tourism Vancouver; Tourism British Columbia.
page 157: Tourism Vancouver; Tourism British Columbia.
page 158: Tourism British Columbia.
page 159: Yukon Government; Yukon Government.
page 160: Yukon Government.
page 161: PAC (c-3805; c-3806).
page 162: Richard Harrington, PAC (pa-129886); Dan Heringa, NWT Economic Development and Tourism; Ojuitok Ipeelee, photo by Richard Beach (taken at the Canadian Museum of Civilization).
page 163: Dan Heringa, NWT Economic Development and Tourism; Irene Tiataalaao, photo by Richard Beach (taken at the Canadian Museum of Civilization).
page 164: Katsunaori Nagase, NWT Economic Development and Tourism.
page 165: Yukon Government.
page 166: Ministère du tourisme du Québec; Gulf Canada Resources Limited; Petroleum Communication Foundation.
page 167: Yukon Government.

UNIT 4

page 168: Ontario Ministry of Tourism and Recreation.
page 170: Dennis Hulbert.

CHAPTER 11

page 172: Canadian Consulate General.
page 173: R. Voom, Canadian Consulate General.
page 174: R. Cooper, Canadian Consulate General.
page 175: Ottawa Tourism and Convention Authority.
page 176: Ottawa Tourism and Convention Authority.
page 178: Canadian Consulate General; United Press Canada Limited.
page 179: Peter Bregg, *Maclean's Magazine*; Canadian Embassy.
page 181: R. Voom, Canadian Consulate General.
page 182: National Film Board of Canada, PAC (pa-150865); National Film Board of Canada, PAC (pa-150867).
page 183: National Film Board of Canada, PAC (pa-150868).

CHAPTER 12

page 184: Dan Heringa, NWT Economic Development and Tourism.
page 185: George Sherman.
page 186: NOVA Corporation of Alberta.
page 187: Ontario Ministry of Tourism and Recreation.
page 188: Hydro-Québec.
page 189: Hydro-Québec.
page 190: Bow Valley Energy, Inc.
page 191: CP, Canadian Consulate General.
page 192: Canadian Consulate General.
page 193: Canadian Government Travel Bureau; Assembly of First Nations.
page 194: George Sherman and Dennis Hulbert.
page 196: Canadian Heritage.
page 197: Canadian Consulate General.
page 199: Canadian Embassy.
page 200: Ministère du tourisme du Québec; Canadian Consulate General.

page 214: Cornelius Krieghoff, PAC (c-10693).
page 224: Ministère du tourisme du Québec.

The first verse of both the French and English versions of the Canadian National Anthem

O CANADA: THE TRUE NORTH

O Canada

O Canada! terre de nos aieux,
Ton front est ceint de fleurons glorieux!
Car ton bras sait porter l'épée,
Il sait porter la croix
Ton histoire est une épopée
Des plus brillants exploits
Et ta valeur de foi trempée,
Protégera nos foyers et nos droits.
Protégera nos foyers et nos droits.

O Canada! Our home and native land!
True patriot love in all thy sons command.
With glowing hearts we see thee rise
The True North strong and free;
From far and wide, O Canada,
We stand on guard for thee.
God keep our land glorious and free!
O Canada, we stand on guard for thee.
O Canada! We stand on guard for thee.

Winter in the Gaspé region of Quebec

with gratitude

We acknowledge the following corporations which have for many years generously supported this and other outreach initiatives of the Center for the Study of Canada

Brascan Ltd.

•

Hiram Walker Group

•

Imasco Ltd.

•

Northern Telecom

•

The Royal Bank of Canada